Fifty-Two Gospel Meditations

by a Modern Pilgrim

Thomas More Press
Chicago, Illinois

Material in this book appeared in different form in the newsletter *Markings* published by the Thomas More Association.

Excerpts from *The Jerusalem Bible,* copyright © 1966 by Darton, Longman & Todd, Ltd. and Doubleday & Company, Inc. Used by permission of the publisher.

ISBN 0-88347 117-5

1

So they hurried away and found Mary and Joseph, and the baby lying in the manger. When they saw the child they repeated what they had been told about him, and everyone who heard it was astonished at what the shepherds had to say. As for Mary, she treasured all these things and pondered them in her heart. And the shepherds went back glorifying and praising God for all they had heard and seen; it was exactly as they had been told.

When the eighth day came and the child was to be circumcised, they gave him the name Jesus, the name the angel had given him before his conception.

Luke 2:16-21

ONE wakes up in the morning, tentatively stretches one's body and then bounds out of bed. The cold is gone, the virus is over; it's no longer necessary to plod through the day at half speed. Life begins again. One peeks out the window. The clouds and the snow, which seem to have lasted all month, have been swept away; the sky is blue and clear and clean, and the sun shines warmly over the face of the earth. We thought the sun would never come back, and finally it has. Life begins again. Or one walks down the steps of the hospital. Strength has returned, the body has healed, the air outside smells good; the colors take on a special glow, and the faces of our family look particularly warm and dear. We have been given a new lease on life. Life begins again. A bitter conflict rages with someone we love. Harsh and hateful words are said, but then sorrow pours out and reconciliation and affection take place. Love arises stronger than ever before. Life begins again. In all these experiences the old, the sick, the decrepit, the hateful, the dull, the monotonous, the routine are swept away and we experience in the depths of our beings the fresh new excitement of beginning again. Life's best moments are its new beginnings.

That's what all the wild, crazy celebration was about last night and, alas, what all the headaches are about this morning. The New Year has always been a time of excitement and wonder for humankind because it is the one time in the course of the cycle of the seasons when we experience a new beginning, a fresh start. New beginnings are such delicious events, such marvelous experiences that we are almost compelled to celebrate even though celebration frequently leaves us with a very old-fashioned headache the next day. The New Year, it often seems, just lasts for a few hours and we are back to the same old monotony and routine. So what if today we have a hangover?

It is not just coincidence but deliberate design on the part of the church that has in recent years turned January 1 into the Feast of Mary at Christmastime. It is really a very old feast, and liturgical reform has brought it back. Mary is the patron saint of new beginnings; she represents the new, the fresh, the exciting, the challenging, the exhilarating, the warm, clean, bright feel of the fresh start. Those reformers who turned against devotion to Mary several hundred years ago did not understand that Mary stood for a new beginning perhaps because many of those whom they criticized did not understand it either. And those Catholics today who have eliminated Mary from their religious lives on the grounds that she is an oldfashioned and unecumenical personage don't understand it either. Paradoxically enough, a number of Protestants and even non-Christian scholars and writers do realize it, and they tell us that Mary is the best part of Catholicism because she symbolizes the rich, powerful, revivifying dynamisms of nature. It is indeed a strange situation when many Catholics seem to be forgetting Mary just at a time when many non-Catholics are rediscovering her. The Catholics are off at their parties in Jerusalem while the non-Catholics, like the shepherds, have come to the crib scene.

Mary reflects for us the vital, life-giving forces at work in the universe. A mother gives life to a child; she brings him into the world, nurses him, keeps him alive through the fragile years of infancy and childhood. When a child is born the human race begins again through him; humanity is given a new opportunity, a new challenge. The shepherds were charmed by the crib scene not because there was anything special about it but because it had the universal charm of a first-born child in the arms of a new mother. The shepherds realized that in that charm there is disclosed to us the universal charm of a God who gives life to all, just as a mother gives life to a child. This was a special child and a special mother, the shepherds knew that much from what they heard on the hilltop.

However, the specialness of the Bethlehem scene did not come because it was isolated from the "fresh start" represented by each new baby that comes into the world. What was special about Bethlehem was that the madonna and child disclosed in a deeper, richer, and more powerful way the revitalizing energies that God showers on his creatures. Jesus and Mary are a new beginning for humankind, a fresh new start, a dawn of a new day, a beginning of an everlasting new year; but they are not cut off or discontinuous or separated from the fresh new beginnings of every birth, every new day, every new year. That feeling of exhilaration, of challenge, of strength that we experience in every new beginning is sustained, revalidated, and confirmed by what happened at Bethlehem and by the scene of the shepherds around the manger. We can then go back to our new beginnings, our fresh new starts, realizing that they are not illusory but that they share in the richness and the significance of Bethlehem; they reveal to us, just as Bethlehem did, how God wants us to live—as though every day were Christmas Day or every day were New Year's—a chance to begin anew, to start all over again.

New Year's resolutions are a joke. We may have said, well, next year we're going to read more, to relax more, or drink less, smoke less, lose weight, or a dozen things we always wanted to do but kept putting off. We know from bitter experience that these resolutions fade quickly. But if we see what the shepherds did at Bethlehem, this is the day to begin anew, to do what we have always wanted to do but have postponed. Today we begin again—and tomorrow, and the day after that, and the one after that, too.

2

After Jesus ·had been born at Bethlehem in Judea during the reign of King Herod, some wise men came to Jerusalem from the east. "Where is the infant king of the Jews?" they asked. "We saw his star as it rose and have come to do him homage." When King Herod heard this he was perturbed, and so was the whole of Jerusalem. He called together all the chief priests and the scribes of the people, and enquired of them where the Christ was to be born. "At Bethlehem in Judaea," they told him "for this is what the prophet wrote:

And you, Bethlehem, in the land of Judah,
you are by no means least among the leaders of Judah,
for out of you will come a leader
who will shepherd my people Israel."

Then Herod summoned the wise men to see him privately. He asked them the exact date on which the star had appeared, and sent them on to Bethlehem. "Go and find out all about the child," he said "and when you have found him, let me know, so that I too may go and do him homage." Having listened to what the king had to say, they set out. And there in front of them was the star they had seen rising; it went forward and halted over the place where the child was. The sight of the star filled them with delight, and going into the house they saw the child with his mother Mary, and falling to their knees they did him homage. Then, opening their treasures, they offered him gifts of gold and frankincense and myrrh. But they were warned in a dream not to go back to Herod, and returned to their own country by a different way.

Matthew 2:1-12

SOME people who write about the Bible have a very interesting interpretation of the gold, frankincense and myrrh that the wise men brought to Jesus, his mother and foster father. They suggest that the wise men were not philosophers or astronomers but really astrologers, magicians, indeed something pretty close to witch doctors; allegedly they used gold, frankincense and myrrh in their witchcraft. They gave the holy family the three gifts as a sign that they were giving up their witchcraft and dedicating themselves to the service of the true God. Whether or not this interpretation is valid, it certainly emphasizes the important point about today's feast: The Epiphany tells us that Jesus came to respond to the religious needs of all humankind, including even those whose religious quest was so misguided that it turned into witchcraft.

One of the great puzzles about the world, at least if we stop to think about it for very long, is the diversity among humankind. It is not merely that God created us in various sizes and shapes with a wide variety of noses, mouths, hair color, natural talents and abilities. He also has created us so that we have vastly different languages, cultures, styles of behavior, and beliefs. If we watch a Balinese dance on television, for example, or see a Buddhist ceremony, or hear people speak in a foreign language, or even go to a church where Mass is being said in a language other than our own, we find ourselves tempted to be suspicious, threatened, hostile, and perhaps a little supercilious. Those people are so different from us, so strange, so peculiar; why can't they be like us? Why can't they be normal, rational, civilized, proper human beings like we are?

Much of the fighting that has gone on through the history of the human race has been over these kinds of differences. We are much more prone to kill people over skin color, language, or religious differences than we are over economic or political ideologies. Indeed, some scholars contend that it is not true that humans are one of the few species to kill their own kind; rather, they say that humans have a very difficult time recognizing their own kind, and the murder of the stranger who dares to be different from us is in fact the murder of somebody who is perceived as someone who does not belong to our species. We probably would not be inclined to kill the Magi should they happen to walk into our neighborhood bar or the country club or the bowling alley our league uses. But we certainly would think them peculiar and it might be wise for someone to call the police. Who are these strange men in their conical hats, their long robes, their forked beards? One of them (is it Melchior?) seems to be of a somewhat different skin color. Well, Magi are all right, maybe, but would you want one living in the house next door? Would you want your sister to marry one?

Note well that it is not the wise men from Jesus' own country but the learned philosophers from Persia or the efficient administrators of Babylon that come to pay him homage. It is barbarians—not exactly savages, perhaps, but certainly thoroughgoing pagans with weird and bizarre beliefs—who come to see Jesus. Doesn't Joseph have any better taste, doesn't Mary have a more developed sense of respectability than to let such peculiar characters wander in? Did Jesus actually come for them, too? Well, if Jesus is compatible with such strange characters from bizarre backgrounds, then he is compatible with just about everyone. And that, indeed, is the theme of the feast of the Epiphany. Jesus came for all humankind precisely because all humankind will find religious fulfillment in him. It is not merely the God-fearing follower of Yahweh who can respond to Jesus but the Zoroastrian (which the Magi probably were), the Buddhist, the Hindu, the animist, the Shintoist, the Moslem, as well as we Western Christians.

For a long time we thought that members of other religions would have to give up everything they believed in and become Christians *just like us* in order to be followers of Jesus of Nazareth. For them salvation would involve a denial of everything in their past and the affirmation of our past. Now we know better. Jesus perfects that which is best in every human religious tradition. Exactly how this works out in practice is sometimes difficult to say, and obviously some things have to change; but if Jesus did not expect the superstitious Magi to give up their heritage (even though they had to give up some of the strange practices in it, such as magic), then he imposes sacrifice of basic culture on nobody. Everything that is good, everything that is true, everything that is rich, everything that is human and inspiring finds its fulfillment in Jesus.

All paths lead to Jesus because he appeals to all. We can see how wrong it was for Western Christians to demand that pagan converts become good Europeans as well as good Christians. Jesus himself would never have made that demand. All that people must do is accept the loving, tender gracious, passionate Father in heaven that Jesus comes to reveal. Everything else can be worked out. It is hard for us to really believe that, of course. We are still suspicious of the foreigner, the stranger, the bizarre visitor. If he wants to become a Christian, he's going to have to become like us. So shave those beards, fellows, get rid of those funny hats, turn in all your sacred books, your holy traditions, your pious devotions and collect your Sunday envelopes and become real Christians like us.

On Epiphany day we must face the fact that we not only have to let into the church those who are different from

10

us; we have to keep the church open to everyone. Some of us would be willing to let in those of a different ethnic background or skin color so long as they practice the faith the way we do, but for us to allow them to keep their own cultures and heritages and to acknowledge that they find fulfillment in Jesus just as we do—well, that pushes the tolerance for many of us pretty far indeed. When the Magi come into our church to pray, they're going to have to take off their hats; we don't pray with our hats on!

3

Then Jesus appeared: he came from Galilee to the Jordan to be baptized by John. John tried to dissuade him. "It is I who need baptism from you" he said "and yet you come to me!" But Jesus replied, "Leave it like this for the time being; it is fitting that we should, in this way, do all that righteousness demands." At this, John gave in to him.

As soon as Jesus was baptized he came up from the water, and suddenly the heavens opened and he saw the Spirit of God descending like a dove and coming down on him. And a voice spoke from heaven, "This is my Son, the Beloved; my favor rests on him."

Matthew 3:13-17

WE all know what it is like to step into a fresh, invigorating shower at the end of a hot, sweaty, wearying summer day. The dirt, the grime, even some of the weariness are swept away by the brisk stream of water. We step out of the shower renewed, ready to take on the responsibilities of the rest of the day. In a small way, the shower waters are a transforming experience.

We drink a cool glass of water when we are thirsty; a rainstorm ends a drought; grime is washed away from our hands; a car goes through the car wash; chocolate is wiped away from a little face; the waters of the lake or ocean pound against the beach—all of these are familiar enough experiences of the cleansing, transforming power of water. For most of us there is not much awareness that water holds the power of life and death over us. If we do not have enough water we die; if we have too much (storms, hurricanes, flooding) we can die. Water is the primal component of the world. Water is so powerful, so important that most people have always thought of it as sacred. Almost every religion the world knows includes some kind of sacred ritual of washing, and the psychologists tell us that water is one of the primal symbols that lurks in our unconscious, standing for life and death, birth and renewal.

Ritual cleansings were quite typical of the Jewish religion in the time of Jesus. Indeed, the Essenes, those strange monks who lived in the torrid and barren monastery on the banks of the Dead Sea, spent a good part of their days going through ritual purifications, renewing themselves spiritually, cleansing themselves of corruption so that they could continue their dedicated lives. John the Baptist was not the first prophet and preacher to come out of the desert to perform a washing ritual as symbol of renewal, of the beginning of a new life of virtue. The washing represented not so much the cleansing away of sins as the commitment of the person washed to begin a new life in which he would attempt to give up his sinful ways.

But why should Jesus be baptized? He was without sin. What need did he have to renew his life? What need did he have to go through a ritual that was certainly understood in his time as a form of penance? We used to say that Jesus was baptized as an act of humility, that even though he was without sin, he still underwent baptism to show his unity with his sinful brothers and sisters, the rest of humankind. Now we understand a deeper meaning in the baptism of Jesus. The ritual washing with water is not only, not even principally, intended to represent penance for sin as it is dedication to a new life. The baptism of Jesus marked a turning point. He had now become a public person. When John the Baptist poured the waters of the Jordan river over him, Jesus formally committed himself to his public work. He dedicated himself to preaching and teaching and healing in the service of his heavenly Father and of the people to whom he had come to bring salvation.

If we understand the baptism of Jesus as a revelation of the power of God through Jesus' commitment of himself to public service, then we have a much better understanding of what our own baptism was like. It too was an inauguration ceremony, the beginning of a life of committed service. Baptism not only removed sin from our soul; more important, it initiated us into the church, and it committed us to a life of service of our fellow human beings. The power of God was manifested in us through this commitment to service just as it was manifested in Jesus through his commitment. When we make our own commitment of the ceremonial one made in our name by our godparents, we become an epiphany, a manifestation of the power of God in the world. The waters of baptism pour over us, cleansing, renewing, refreshing, dedicating but also revealing the goodness and the love of God that has been poured into our personalities.

Each year at Easter we renew our baptismal vows, and every time we make the sign of the cross (with or without holy water) we are in fact reenacting the ceremony of our baptism. We remind ourselves again and again that we are dedicated to the service of the Trinity. The sign of the cross is a spiritual version of what used to be said of Coca-Cola, "the pause that refreshes." We need daily spiritual renewal and refreshment; we need to rededicate and recommit ourselves each day to our vocation of being manifestations of God's love.

We should try each day to make the sign of the cross

not as a hasty, thoughtless, almost superstitious gesture but as a meaningful statement of what we believe in, of who we know we are, and to what we have committed our lives. We can imagine that the waters of baptism are flowing again, bringing us new life and manifesting to and within us the power of God, whose child we really are and who is truly well-pleased with what we are trying to do.

4

*The next day, seeing Jesus coming toward him, John said,
"look, there is the lamb of God that takes away the sin of
the world. This is the one I spoke of when I said: A man
is coming after me who ranks before me because he existed
before me. I did not know him myself, and yet it was to
reveal him to Israel that I came baptizing with water."
John also declared, "I saw the Spirit coming down on him
from heaven like a dove and resting on him. I did not
know him myself, but he who sent me to baptize with
water had said to me, 'The man on whom you see the
Spirit come down and rest is the one who is going to baptize with the Holy Spirit.' Yes, I have seen and I am the
witness that he is the Chosen One of God."*

John 1:29-34

WE are walking down a crowded street, or through a de-
partment store, or waiting on a subway platform or at a
bus stop, or perhaps walking through an airport filled with
people at holiday time. We notice that there is something
vaguely familiar about another person in the crowd—a
tilt of the head, a style of walk, the swing of shoulders, the
tone of voice. Somewhere, sometime in our past we have
known this person. We dig deep in our memory. The other
person seems puzzled by us, as though he/she is also in a
moment of prerecognition. Sometimes the light dawns simultaneously. Of course, we remember this person from
childhood, teen years, or young adult years. How much
they have changed and how much they have remained the

same. Other times the recognition never quite comes. We have confused the mysterious stranger with someone else. Still other times it is an eerie *deja vu* experience. We have never known the other before, and yet, somehow, we are almost positive we have seen him/her. So we may have a real recognition, a false recognition, or a mysterious recognition. Such experiences are always disconcerting because they touch deep down into the hidden memories of our past.

The recognition experience can take other forms. Husbands and wives will admit sometimes that the first time they saw their future spouse enter a room they knew instantly that this was the person they would marry. Other times we can tell when we meet a person whether that person will be a friend or not. There is something indefinable in the way he/she smiles or talks, the instantaneous revelation of interests, commitments, values—we simply *know* that this other will be a friend, though it will take a long time to articulate precisely the grounds of the friendship.

Psychologists tell us that in all these "recognition experiences" the "preconscious" is at work. This aspect of our personality is something like a radar scanner which collects data far more rapidly than we can evaluate it. Sometimes the impression from this built-in radar set is so powerful that even without our having to evaluate we simply know when someone is "our kind" of person. (For what it's worth, the "preconscious" is the same thing as the *intellectus agens* of our old Scholastic philosophy courses.) Sometimes the preconscious is wrong, we didn't know the other person at all. But, too, it is often right; it has "eyes" to see that are incredibly powerful.

Obviously it is one of these "recognition experiences" that is described in St. John's Gospel account of John the

Baptist's recognition and proclamation of Jesus as the Lamb of God. The experience is heavily laden with theological reflections of the evangelist and with religious symbols; yet what is described is a kind of psychological experience that we often have: Jesus had been a disciple of John's for some time; John knew him, he had even baptized him. But then, suddenly, all the pieces of the "Jesus puzzle" fit together for the Baptist in a profound moment of recognition. The remarkable young man, so pleasant, so intelligent, so principled, so patient, and yet so strong and vigorous, had always seemed to the Baptist to be someone "special." Now the precise nature of that "specialness" in Jesus was evident; he was the one who was to come, the one for whom the Baptist had been preparing. All the parts fit together; the puzzle was solved. John the Baptist *knew* who Jesus was.

There are two kinds of recognition when we suddenly see all the pieces of the Jesus puzzle fit together for ourselves. We understand what he is talking about, we grasp for the first time the full burden of his message, we perceive his point of view, we get, as it were, "inside his head," and see the world the way he saw it. The moment of recognition can be a kind of "conversion" experience or a form of "twice born" experience of which some of our Protestant and even Catholic charismatic brothers and sisters speak. But it need not be that powerful or that dramatic. It is simply an experience of understanding what Jesus is talking about finally and fully and deciding that we are willing to take a chance on living that way, living lives of trust, openness, of courage, generosity.

The second form of recognition experience is to discover Jesus in someone else. It is often the result of the first experience, for if one fully understands the message of Jesus, then one also perceives that one must love the brothers and the sisters as though they were Jesus. So, whatever we do to them we do to Jesus. This second sort of recognition experience reveals to us a particular person who merits our kindness, our patience, and our love just as though he/she were Jesus himself. Or it is a particular situation which demands from us passionate concern, just as though it were Jesus himself who was suffering in the situation. If we pay attention to our "recognition experience," our lives are transformed and so is the life of the other person.

One of the troubles with recognition experiences is that they are fleeting. They are instantaneous insights which can be lost quickly, indeed, hardly even noticed. We are so busy with so many things, so preoccupied with our responsibilities, our duties, our problems, so worried about our concerns, so eager to meet the schedules and deadlines of our daily life. Our recognition experience can be like a blinding explosion, a sudden flash of light; in its intensity we see, but it is gone so quickly that we can persuade ourselves we never saw. Yet it is a fair bet that in each of our lives during the past week there was at least one such moment of recognition when we saw a person or a truth clearly and decisively. What did we do about that experience? Did we act upon it? Did we see it as enthusiastically as John the Baptist did? Or did we let it drift away, affecting our lives not at all—as though it never occurred?

5

Hearing that John had been arrested he went back to Galilee, and leaving Nazareth he went and settled in Capernaum, a lakeside town on the borders of Zebulun and Naphtali. In this way the prophecy of Isaiah was to be fulfilled:

Land of Zebulun! Land of Naphtali!
Way of the sea on the far side of Jordan,
Galilee of the nations!
The people that lived in darkness
has seen a great light;
on those who dwell in the land and shadow of death
a light has dawned.

From that moment Jesus began his preaching with the message, "Repent, for the kingdom of heaven is close at hand."

As he was walking by the Sea of Galilee he saw two brothers, Simon, who was called Peter, and his brother Andrew; they were making a cast in the lake with their net, for they were fishermen. And he said to them, "Follow me and I will make you fishers of men." And they left their nets at once and followed him.

Going on from there he saw another pair of brothers, James son of Zebedee and his brother John; they were in their boat with their father Zebedee, mending their nets, and he called them. At once, leaving the boat and their father, they followed him.

He went round the whole of Galilee teaching in their synagogues, proclaiming the Good News of the kingdom and curing all kinds of diseases and sicknesses among the people.

Matthew 4:12-23

LET us suppose that you are a pagan who has lived isolated in the jungle for all your life. Somehow or other (perhaps from Tarzan and Jane), you have learned how to read. You have come across the New Testament and have heard the message of Jesus. The light that Jesus has brought into the world dawns on you and you say to yourself, "Aha! I shall leave the darkness of the jungle, follow the light of Christ, and become a Christian." So you depart from the jungle and come to a clearing where there is a town. You ask one of the townspeople where the Christian church is. When the native recovers from the shock of your jungle-determined appearance, he asks you, "Which Christian church do you mean? Baptist? Methodist? Congregational? Pentecostal? Or the Roman Catholic, Lutheran, Evangelical?" You shake your head. "No, I want the Christian church," you say. "But," says the native, "they all are Christian churches. Which one do you want?" You think about that for a moment. Finally you excuse yourself and go back to the jungle and think it all over. The way you read the book, there was only one Christian church.

There is only one good reason for fighting with other human beings: We have to get them before they get us. No one ever admits even to himself that he is the aggressor. We always act with hostility in self-defense. We love peace and hate conflict. If only other people would leave us alone, would not threaten us, harass us, hassle us, there would be nothing but peace. We are peace-loving people, and we fight only because our war-loving fellows force us to it. We go down the river to wipe out the enemy village because we are convinced that if we don't, they will get to us first. Sure enough, as we go down the warpath, we may well meet the raiding party coming to get us before we get them.

It is critically important to understand that in the gospels the emphasis is on the universality of the good news that Jesus is preaching. Salvation is for everyone, not just for the Jews, not just for the citizens of Capernaum but for everyone—even the pagans. Christianity is not to be an exclusivist religion. No one, whatever his nationality or language, race or cultural background is to be barred admission to the church. Indeed, one of the perennial problems for Christians has been a temptation to equate their own civilization and culture with Christianity. In the early days you could only become a Christian, it was thought, if you became a Jew; in our own time much missionary effort seemed to assume that if an Asian or an African wanted to become a Christian he also had to become a European. Much of the conflict and dissension that has kept Christians at odds with one another (even on occasion killing one another) was based on the conviction that there was only one possible way to be a Christian—their own way. Everyone else who disagreed with them was a heretic if not an infidel. In our own ecumenical age we are more tolerant perhaps. We are ready to let the light of Jesus shine wherever it may; but still our resentment toward those who are different from us can be very powerful. Why don't they see the light the same way we see it?

We should pray for the unity which only God's grace and love can give. It is our fighting and feuding, our fears, anger and hatreds that have kept the darkness and the misery that has impeded the joyous celebration and dimmed the light that Christ brought into the world. It is our suspicion, distrust, envy, animosity which has interferred with the glories proclaimed in the gospel. People in the past created disunity, but we have continued. It is disunity not only among those who are in the various denominations but also among those who are Catholics, indeed even among those who are part of one parish or one family. It is only in a life of service that we reveal the light that Jesus brought into the world. If our lives are full of conflict and disunity, we snuff out the light of Jesus. We are like reflecting mirrors; only when they are highly polished can the light get into the nooks and crannies, the caves and ravines of the deep valleys. We either bring light to the world or we make the darkness worse.

It will do no good to pray for unity among Christians if we do not at the same time try to heal the wounds which keep light out of our personal relationships and make them dark and miserable. The best way to facilitate unity among Christians is to bring joy and celebration and light into our own personal lives.

6

*Then he began to speak to them, "This text is being ful-
filled today even as you listen." And he won the approval
of all, and they were astonished by the gracious words that
came from his lips.*

*They said, "This is Joseph's son, surely?" But he replied,
"No doubt you will quote me the saying, 'Physician, heal
yourself' and tell me, 'We have heard all that happened in
Capernaum, do the same here in your own countryside.' "
And he went on, "I tell you solemnly, no prophet is ever
accepted in his own country.*

*"There were many widows in Israel, I can assure you, in
Elijah's day, when heaven remained shut for three years
and six months and a great famine raged throughout the
land, but Elijah was not sent to any one of these: he was
sent to a widow at Zarephath, a Sidonian town. And in
the prophet Elisha's time there were many lepers in Israel,
but none of these was cured, except the Syrian, Naaman."*

*When they heard this everyone in the synagogue was
enraged. They sprang to their feet and hustled him out of
the town; and they took him up to the brow of the hill
their town was built on, intending to throw him down the
cliff, but he slipped through the crowd and walked away.*

Luke 4:21-30

AN experience which is bound to bring back unpleasant
memories from our past is to hear a little child say to another little child, "We aren't going to play with you any
more because we don't *like* you!" Few of us have escaped

those words during our childhood. They came on us like an avalanche. We thought we were getting along fine with our friends, and suddenly, without warning, they all turned against us and excluded us—usually when we had done something rather special or important or impressive, like being the only one in the class to get an A on a test, or the first one on the block to ride down the street on a "two-wheeler." We may have suppressed the memory, but we learned the lesson: Don't get too far ahead. There is no more deadly weapon than envy. And we see it at work in the gospel story of Jesus being thrown out of town by his own friends and townsfolk. It was a preview of Calvary, for if your friends don't support you, who will?

To be rejected is a devastating experience. A friend turns against us; a favorite teacher is unfair to us; we work up enough nerve to ask for a date and get a flat no; we try to have a party and no one can come; we make an overture toward friendship and are ignored; we offer a gift and it is scarcely noticed; we work hard on a good dinner and no one seems to enjoy it—great or small, experiences of rejection hurt, and they particularly hurt when they come from those we love. They most particularly hurt when the basic reason for the rejection is envy, when our loved ones turn against us because we do well. Envy would kill if it could, it would kill the goodness in us, the excellence; and if the matter is serious enough, it can actually destroy our physical life. The townsfolk of Nazareth threw Jesus out of the town and maybe planned to kill him; eventually, other enemies did kill him. Envy is the great, dirty, ugly secret of humankind; it is one of the most powerful of human motivations, perhaps the most powerful after hunger and sex. Certainly it is the most evil of the propensities of the human personality. Oddly enough, while we all know the experience of being the object of envy, we are not thereby prevented from envying others. No matter how painful, how devastating it is to be envied, we are not inhibited one bit from envying others. Envy is a disease that does not create immunity in its victims.

There are two lessons from Luke's Gospel and both are difficult. The first lesson is that no matter how powerful the rejection, no matter how deep the pain imposed by envy, we must not give in to its sanctions. He who settles for spiritual or human mediocrity because he fears envy will have a dull, third-rate life. Jesus could easily quit when his friends and townsfolk turned against him; he could have said, "Why bother? I did my best, I preached my Good News to them; they didn't want to listen. So if my friends and neighbors won't listen to me, who will? Why waste my time bringing Good News to those who don't want to hear it?" Those are sentiments with which we are all too familiar. We have often quit because others have turned against us when we have done something good, something generous, something that represents the best of our talents and abilities. We feel like saying, "To heck with it. If that's the way they're going to react, I'm not going to waste my time trying to do something worthwhile for them. I'll settle down and lead a quiet, dull life, and that'll show 'em; it will be their hard luck."

But, of course, it's our hard luck if we settle for being just "ordinary" because others will envy us if we are better than ordinary, if we try harder, live longer, pray more, give more of ourselves. The great men and women who have become social, political, religious, or economic leaders have suffered terribly because of envy. But they would have suffered more if they permitted envy to restrict or constrain their talents and abilities. So, too, with all of us. If we do our best and try our hardest, then we shall certainly suffer other's envy; but if we don't, we shall suffer mediocrity, and in the long run, that makes life even more intolerable. Jesus did not quit when faced with the sanctions imposed on him for excellence; and neither should those who claim to be his followers.

Jesus did not quit precisely because he knew that even if his friends and neighbors turned against him, he still had the Heavenly Father's love. God loves us, and when it seems that we are rejected by almost everyone else, we can turn to God and know that there is love, reassurance, and respect for what we try to do. Jesus went on after Nazareth because he knew about God's love; so must we when envy threatens to destroy our enthusiasms. Rarely in life will we have to face a situation where we are completely alone without any human support. Normally God supports both directly and indirectly through our loved ones and friends who remain loyal; but even in those rare instances when we are all by ourselves, we are still not alone.

The other lesson from Luke's gospel is that if we are, all of us, victims of envy, so we will victimize others with envy. It is quite easy to identify with Jesus at the edge of the hill in Nazareth, but if we are honest with ourselves, we must face the fact that all too frequently we are on the other side—with the townsfolk who revile him and force him out of town by trying to force him off the edge of the hill. Frequently we cut others down to size, ask them, "Who do you think you are?", punish those who are a challenge to our own mediocrity. The success, the good works, the talents and gifts of others are an unjustified oppression for the envious. It is not merely that we would like to do what others have done and have what they have; we also would like to deprive them of what they have and destroy what they have done. Envy is the motivating force behind most assassinations, and even though there are few Lee

Harvey Oswalds, Sirhan Sirhans, and James Earl Rays in the country, the emotion that was pathologically destructive in them is strong in all of us. Yes, go on. Push him over the cliff!

How much of what we do is caused by envy? We fear the envy of others or desire to punish those whom we envy. In each of our lives is it really true that envy is the third most powerful emotion?

7

"You are the salt of the earth. But if salt becomes tasteless, what can make it salty again? It is good for nothing, and can only be thrown out to be trampled underfoot by men.

"You are the light of the world. A city built on a hill-top cannot be hidden. No one lights a lamp to put it under a tub; they put it on the lamp-stand where it shines for everyone in the house. In the same way your light must shine in the sight of men, so that, seeing your good works, they may give the praise to your Father in heaven."

Matthew 5:13-16

THE poet Goethe said: "The world is so empty if one thinks only of mountains, rivers, and cities; but to know someone who thinks and feels with us and, though distant, is close to us in spirit, this makes the earth for us an inhabited garden." To be close to someone else in spirit, to think and feel with someone else, to make the earth into an inhabited garden for someone else, that is how we who are followers of Jesus become the salt of the earth and the light of the world.

It often seems when we look at our lives that we receive a lot more help from other people than we give. In moments of searching honesty we realize how much we are indebted to our parents, our families, our teachers, our spouses, our friends. Yet we must not leave out the fact that often we are on the giving end of things too. We help another person prepare for a test; we counsel a friend who is confused, dubious, uncertain; we are patient and kind with a sick parent; we tolerate an annoying neighbor; we listen sensitively to the fears of a child; we open ourselves in warm sympathy to someone who is suffering; we say just the right word, touch a hand with just the right affection when the one we love is troubled, anxious, insecure. The cliche that it is better to give than to receive has been overused to the point of emptiness, and yet in moments of tenderness, sensitivity, and patience we know that giving is very good indeed. We find ourselves wondering why we don't give more.

Maybe the reason we do not give more is that we have so little confidence in what there is inside us to give. Self-rejection, low self-esteem, self-hatred, self-deprecation are widespread and not frequently denounced sins. It is false humility—every bit as evil as pride—to think that we are worthless, that we have nothing to offer, that there is in us no goodness that can overflow and touch the hearts of others. Sometimes we minimize our own goodness as an excuse for not being generous to others; but more often, it is to be feared, we really are persuaded that we can give little because we have little, that there is nothing for us to do to help others because there is nothing of any value or merit inside ourselves.

As light and salt are indispensable for human existence, so, too, are we. Our lives become important, not because of our own goodness or virtue or merit but rather because we have been chosen to reflect the light of the world, which is Jesus, and to spread the salt of the earth, which is God's love. The ordinary response to the vocation to be salt and light is to compromise. We say, in effect: "Isn't it okay if I provide only medium quality salt and moderately bright light? How about leading a life that is a little bit out of the ordinary, but not so different that everyone can recognize instantly what I am? Can't I accept my vocation as a

Christian but still not be embarrassed by it?" We would like to make a deal with Jesus: Other people would provide most of the light and most of the salt and we would be only too happy to help them.

The clarion cry the gospel words, "You are the salt of the earth, you are the light of the world," strikes us with the same renewing power as a cup of coffee in mid-morning, a day off after a weary week, perhaps a brief winter vacation in the sunshine. It energizes us, turns us on, releases our natural goodness, encourages us to begin giving once again because, after all, we are good, we are marvelous, we are wonderful, we are lovable, we can do good for other human beings.

Note well what Jesus says in the gospel: You are the light of the world and the salt of the earth, not that you *will become* so, or that someday you *might be,* or that *eventually* it might turn out that you will act like this. No, you *are.* The apostles, who were just average men like us, must have wondered what made them suddenly salt of the earth and light of the world. The answer is that their own native, creative goodness, transformed by their contact with the saving mission of Jesus, was the operative force.

When our own natural attractiveness is reinforced by the joy of believing that God is love, that life is good, that love conquers hate, and that life triumphs over death, we become the light of the world; and our own natural abilities and talents are illumined by the powerful, glowing light of the Good News that Jesus came to preach. Be clear about it: It is not just our natural goodness, but it is not just the gospel either; it is the combination of the two which gives us the extraordinary and tremendous ability we have to bring joy and happiness to the lives of others.

Jesus' words are obviously intended to be taken as encouragement, reassurance, rejuvenation. We are warned, of course, that the salt can lose its savor; and we are told that some foolish people hide their lights under bushels. Nevertheless, Matthew's gospel is designed to make us "look up and live," to lift up our hearts, to hold our heads high, to walk forth with a confident and steady step. There is so much good we can do, so much joy we can bring, so much love we can offer. The challenge of this gospel is to ask ourselves again, who needs our love? Who can be turned on again to the taste of our salt and bathe in the warm, glowing light of our love?

8

A leper came to him and pleaded on his knees: "If you want to" he said "you can cure me." Feeling sorry for him, Jesus stretched out his hand and touched him. "Of course I want to!" he said. "Be cured!" And the leprosy left him at once and he was cured. Jesus immediately sent him away and sternly ordered him, "Mind you say nothing to anyone, but go and show yourself to the priest, and make the offering for your healing prescribed by Moses as evidence of your recovery." The man went away, but then started talking about it freely and telling the story everywhere, so that Jesus could no longer go openly into any town, but had to stay outside in places where nobody lived. Even so, people from all around would come to him.

Mark 1:40-45

AS far as minor inconveniences go, having to spend time in a place designed for air conditioning when it doesn't work must be one of the worst. In the old buses and trains, if the air conditioning conked out in the middle of the summer, or if there was a sudden hot day early in spring or late in the fall, all you had to do was open the windows. Now you suffer in agony. Similarly, there are a lot of office buildings and not a few churches built with windows no one can open; that's fine, when the air conditioning works, but when it breaks down you get a strong hint of what purgatory must be like. Any more than a few minutes in one of these man-made infernos and you become sticky, smelly, dirty, contentious, difficult, impatient, and then furious. Every extra minute you are denied the cleansing pleasures of a shower seems an added affront to human integrity and dignity. Maybe we moderns are obsessed with cleanliness; maybe it doesn't make any difference, as some of the hippies tell us, if you are dirty and smelly. Be that as it may, when you finally escape, the soothing waters of a shower seem like a foretaste of heaven after purgatory.

Mark, the author of the oldest gospel was concerned about the superstitions he saw growing up alongside Christian devotion to Jesus. Mark knew how the popular mind devours tales of the occult, the strange, the marvelous; and he vigorously resisted the propensity of his contemporaries to see Jesus as just one more product of the occult "counterculture" of the Roman Empire. Hence, Mark was very careful to link his account of the marvels of Jesus to religious teaching. He took the story that was available to him of the cleansing of a leper and used it to present Jesus not merely as a healer but a healer of the basic human affliction of sinfulness. Leprosy in the physical world, says Mark, is what sinfulness is in the spiritual world. Jesus cleansed people of their leprosy, indeed, but such a marvelous event was merely a sign of a far more important, a far more wonderful power Jesus had to heal us of our sins. "Pay attention," he told his own readers—and us, too, for that matter—"to the really important things about Jesus: he cleanses us of our sinfulness."

The hot, sticky, dirty feeling we have while we are cooped up, with no air conditioning, during a long train or bus ride can be the physical equivalent for us, who know rather little about leprosy, of the spiritual experience of sin. The refreshing blast of the air conditioning when it finally starts working can be not unlike the revivifying touch of forgiveness that Jesus offers for our sinfulness. There is no doubt that we are sinners, that we are born sinful; that is to say, we were born into a human race that has sinful proclivities and predispositions. We inherit from our parents certain physiological and cultural weaknesses; we acquire defense mechanisms, neurotic escapes, prejudices, biases, personal limitations in our early childhood experiences. Our social class, our geographical environment impose more limitations on us, and then, as though all the sinful propensities of our heritage are not enough, we set about acquiring new sinful tendencies of our own— habits of dishonesty, exploitation, cruelty, laziness, insensitivity, self-indulgence, blaming others, punishing others, nastiness, vindictiveness, and a whole host of faults, vices, bad habits and other moral and spiritual weaknesses, major and minor. If we don't at least occasionally feel the vile filth of our own sinfulness, then we have no moral or religious sensitivity left.

Spiritually, we are dirty, sweaty, smelly, offensive. It has not been fashionable for a long time to talk much about our sinfulness. Recently, some authors, like Karl Menninger, have been asking, "Whatever happened to sin?" The answer is that it has been around all the time; we have just been too busy—and prettied ourselves up too much with false deodorants—to notice how bad we really are. We are not irredeemably bad, of course; but still, we are bad enough. There are very few of us who can look at our lives and feel proud of our record of virtue. If the final judgment really were a time when all our hidden faults were to be revealed (as may have been hinted to us in grammar school), then most of us would be strongly inclined to call in sick on the day of that glorious event. Indeed, when we stop to think of the kind of lives we have lived—the good we haven't done and the bad we have; the things we ought not to have done that we did, and the things we ought to have done that we didn't—we might be forced to conclude that we are in fact moral lepers.

The man who presented himself to Jesus in Mark's gospel had a physical ailment that occasionally the natural forces of nature cured and which, nowadays, wonder drugs would clear up quickly and effectively. For Jesus to cure him was impressive but not completely unusual; so, too, moral leprosy, moral guilt, is no more easy to cure today than it was in the time of Jesus. The forgiveness of sins is every bit as much pure grace now as it was then.

It is easy to be paralyzed but our moral ugliness. In school, perhaps, we heard of the sin of despair, that ultimate and unforgivable fault of those who thought they were so bad that even God couldn't forgive them. Although we never thought we'd be *that* big a sinner, there is something rather equivalent to despair; it is very easy to be so fed up with one's own faults, frailties and mistakes, and with one's own petty indifferences, insensitivities and cruelties as to stop trying and become a moral zombie, drifting through life, responding to the pressures of external circumstances because we have really given up all hope of asserting responsible control over our own lives. Yet, if Jesus really heals our moral guilt, if he really cleanses us from the leprosy of sinfulness, then we are held to start all over again, we are bound to begin trying once more, we are obliged to attempt to control our own moral lives, we are under constraints to strive to eliminate petty, nasty, viciousness that is so much a part of our personalities. Sometimes it seems easier to remain leprous.

Lent is a time of penance and a time of transformation, a time of 180 degree turn. We should begin to think about what particular and special kind of moral ugliness makes us most obnoxious to our family, our friends, our coworkers, those who know us well. What should we stop doing if we really believed that God is ready and willing to cure us of our sin, just as Jesus was ready to cure the leper in the gospel?

9

Filled with the Holy Spirit, Jesus left the Jordan and was led by the Spirit through the wilderness, being tempted there by the devil for forty days. During that time he ate nothing and at the end he was hungry. Then the devil said to him, "If you are the Son of God, tell this stone to turn into a loaf." But Jesus replied, "Scripture says: Man does not live on bread alone."

Then leading him to a height, the devil showed him in a moment of time all the kingdoms of the world and said to him, "I will give you all this power and the glory of these kingdoms, for it has been committed to me and I give it to anyone I choose. Worship me, then, and it shall all be yours." But Jesus answered him, "Scripture says: You must worship the Lord your God, and serve him alone."

Then he led him to Jerusalem and made him stand on the parapet of the Temple. "If you are the Son of God," he said to him "throw yourself down from here, for scripture says: He will put his angels in charge of you to guard you. And again: They will hold you up on their hands in case you hurt your foot against a stone." But Jesus answered him, "It has been said: You must not put the Lord your God to the test."

Having exhausted all these ways of tempting him, the devil left him, to return at the appointed time.

Luke 4:1-13

FIFTY-TWO GOSPEL MEDITATIONS

THERE could not be a better time of the year to meditate on the account of Jesus' temptation in the Wilderness (Luke 4:1-13). For this is the time when most of us have a bad case of the blahs. The holidays have receded into the past, and in much of the country spring is still a long way in the future. A lot of us have the sniffles, some of us have a low-level sinus or bronchial infection that's gone on for weeks now and will probably go on forever. Life is gray—the sky is gray, the ground is gray, where there is snow, it's gray and dirty. We are in a rut; hours, days, weeks blend into one another in dismal monotony. We are tired, discouraged, weary; it's still a long, long time until Easter. We are able to understand, if we stop to think about it, how Jesus felt in the wilderness. He, too, was weary; he, too had the blahs just when Satan appeared to trick him.

The temptation of Jesus, we are told by those who study the Bible, was a temptation to "cheat," to win the cooperation of people by magic and marvel, by tricks and games, to force people to join the band of his followers by the wonders of his miraculous powers. But this was not God's "game plan"; people were to become followers of Jesus not because he was a wonder worker but because he spoke the truth, not because they were charmed by the spectaculars he performed for them but because they were charmed by the loving, gracious God for whom he claimed to speak. People were not to be high-pressured by signs and marvels; they were to be attracted by beauty and love, and to make their own free choice about following his attractions. The temptation of Jesus, then, was a temptation to take a short cut, to cheat a little, to deprive people of some of their freedom of choice by relying on special tricks instead of God's loving goodness for attracting people into the kingdom.

It is an understandable temptation, and one that the leaders of the Christian church have not always avoided themselves. The Christian faith was so important, membership in the church so essential for salvation—or so it seemed—that it became appropriate to use short cuts, to "lead" people into the church (for their own good, of course) by various signs and wonders. If there were no miracles available or spectacular works to compel assent, well, they could always fall back on baptizing the king and bringing the whole people in with him, or on feeding rice to the hungry, or even building hospitals and schools to attract the suffering and ignorant. And if people hesitated, you could use the Inquisition and call in the secular arm. Mind you, it was all for their own good; in the absence of a free act of commitment or in the slowness of people making that free act, one could use force, fear, marvels, guilt, or even generous services—for their own good, of course. And then came the convert-makers, people with high-pressure sales and advertising techniques who kept track of the number of converts they had made or of the hundreds and even thousands they had baptized. The church was expanding, was it not? The Kingdom of God was growing, was it not? What did it matter if a few little short cuts were taken now and then. Oh, yes, it's a very easy temptation to understand.

Many scripture texts used in Lenten liturgies stress faith. Faith in these readings does not mean the acceptance of certain specified doctrinal propositions but something much more basic and fundamental: Faith here is the belief in God's loving goodness based on the free act by which the whole personality of the human being is committed definitively and irrevocably to respond to that loving goodness.

Just as there are many easy short cuts by which people try to compel faith, so there many easy short cuts for the act of faith. We try to hedge our bets by equating faith with keeping the rules—going to church, obeying the laws, playing the game the way it ought to be played; or we try to equate faith with hatred for those whom we deem to be God's enemies. We become militant crusaders or scrupulous law-abiders, because crusading against enemies and keeping the minutiae of the rules are both much easier than loving commitment in response to a loving invitation. So much of the history of Christianity has been marked by phony faith responding to phony signs and wonders. The freedom of God's invitation and the freedom of our response get lost in all the fakery.

Faith is not a single act that, once made, eliminates all difficulties. Just as the loving union between a man and woman in marriage is a commitment continuously renewed in each day of their common life despite faults, failings, hesitancies, doubts, and even apparent temporary withdrawals of commitment, so, too, our commitment to God and faith must always be renewed—sometimes in the face of great obstacles and difficulties. The honest Christian, just like the honest married lover, knows how weak and insecure he or she is, and takes confidence not so much in the strength of his or her faith but rather in the determination to keep trying; the Christian does his or her best, and the rest depends on the strength of God. God in his goodness will send angels to minister to the Christian after the exhausting effort of overcoming temptation, just as angels were sent to Jesus in the desert.

Our act of faith, then, is a free act. Nobody can constrain us to make it and no amount of faking can substitute for it. During Lent, let us examine our faith. How strong is it? How consistent, how honest, how free, and how much of it is fake, phony, a cheat? Because faith is hard, have we fallen to the Devil's temptation and taken a short cut? Do we really believe, and do we really try to live as though we believe the whole of our lives are somehow or other transformed by God's loving goodness? Or are we cheating, faking, frauding?

10

FIFTY-TWO GOSPEL MEDITATIONS

Six days later, Jesus took with him Peter and James and John and led them up a high mountain where they could be alone by themselves. There in their presence he was transfigured: his clothes became dazzlingly white, whiter than any earthly bleacher could make them. Elijah appeared to them with Moses; and they were talking with Jesus. Then Peter spoke to Jesus: "Rabbi," he said "it is wonderful for us to be here; so let us make three tents, one for you, one for Moses and one for Elijah." He did not know what to say; they were so frightetned. And a cloud came, covering them in shadow; and there came a voice from the cloud, "this is my Son, the Beloved. Listen to him." Then suddenly, when they looked round, they saw no one with them any more but only Jesus.

As they came down from the mountain he warned them to tell no one what they had seen, until after the Son of Man had risen from the dead.

Mark 9:2-10

THERE are occasions in the life of each of us when time stands still, when the whole world seems to rush in upon us benignly and graciously, when we find ourselves caught up in emotions of great peace and joy, when we see the unity of everything in the universe, when warmth and happiness seem to fill us to the brim and overflow. These brief interludes of peace and joy may be almost unbearably powerful or they may be very light and gentle; they may be a deep "mystical" experience or merely a pleasant, quiet interlude that catches us unawares. These transient episodes, which usually just "happen," show us hints of what life is all about; but it doesn't last, and even while we reach out to hold it tighter, the brief moment, when our lives and everything that has happened to us seem to make sense, recedes.

The transfiguration of Jesus was an overwhelmingly powerful version of those little interludes of peace and joy we all experience in our lives, those transient interludes when we see exactly what our lives are all about and what we must do if we are to be true to ourselves. For most of us these "religious experiences" are not very powerful and do not give dominant tone and direction to our lives, though for some people (perhaps a quarter of the population), according to recent statistics, these experiences are very powerful and very important. For most of us they are merely a hint of an explanation, but for some they are a road map with the path marked out from which they are unable to deviate.

Such was the experience of Jesus in the transfiguration. His public life was drawing to a close, he knew he had done just about all he could to preach the Good News of his heavenly Father's Kingdom. Now something else awaited him to finish his mission, but as far as human knowledge was concerned it was not yet fully clear what had to be done. On Mount Tabor, in the midst of the overwhelmingly powerful transfiguration experience, it became clear to Jesus what he had to do. He had to go up to Jerusalem and suffer and die for the Kingdom he was preaching. The Tabor experience was one of joy and glory, but it was also an overwhelmingly powerful command to Jesus. He must go up to Jerusalem and die.

For the early Christians the circle was complete. In his moment of glory, Jesus saw that he must die, but his death

43

in its turn would produce the final glory of the resurrection. The transfiguration was both the anticipation of Easter and the command to go forward to Good Friday. Mark, arguing as he does throughout his gospel against those who wish to turn Jesus into nothing more than a worker of marvels, strongly emphasizes that the glory of the transfiguration experience should be kept secret until after the death and resurrection of Jesus. One could only understand Tabor, in other words, in light of Calvary, because Calvary links Tabor to Easter. Jesus had to come down from the mountain, enter the depths of human suffering in order that he might finally rise up.

There is a profound psychological and human truth in this insight. We must suffer before we can exult. In the ordinary experiences of growth in our daily lives, we only become better human beings by dying to a part of ourselves. The close relationship between a husband and wife, for example, can only expand and grow into a deeper and richer love if man and woman are willing to die to their selfish defensive, punitive, vindictive, impatient inclinations. Marriage begins with a transfiguration experience. A married couple go down into a valley of suffering together before they can come up on the other side and experience even greater joy than at the beginning of their marriage. This cycle of joy and suffering and then greater joy goes on frequently, sometimes even daily, in their life together.

So it is with us. Our lives offer us frequent interludes of joy—little Tabors if not big ones—and in these interludes we catch hints of the great joy that seems to be beckoning us and calling to us. But then the interlude passes and the monotony, the heartache, the routine and the anxieties of life return. We must ask ourselves whether the interludes of joy or the interludes of sorrow are the better hint of what life is all about. There is no way any of us can escape suffering in this life; the issue is whether we bear it bravely as an interlude and even a cause of our subsequent joy, or whether we rebel against it and try to avoid entering the valley of sorrow. Eventually we all enter that valley; we all die. The question is *how* will we die?

The research of Elisabeth Kubler-Ross on those who are resuscitated after "death" would indicate that all experience transfiguration-like episodes as the moment of death. Some resent being pulled back into life, and none of them, she tells us, are ever afraid to die again. Dr. Kubler-Ross says that she is convinced now, as a matter of scientific certainty, that death does not end life. This certainly follows the parallel path of the Christian conviction that life and death and more life are inextricably related. As the poet Francis Thompson says: "Death and birth are inseparable upon the earth, for they are twain yet one, and death is birth."

11

Just before the Jewish Passover Jesus went up to Jerusalem, and in the Temple he found people selling cattle and sheep and pigeons, and the money changers sitting at their counters there. Making a whip out of some cord, he drove them all out of the Temple, cattle and sheep as well, scattered the money changers' coins, knocked their tables over and said to the pigeon-sellers, "Take all this out of here and stop turning my Father's house into a market." Then his disciples remembered the words of scripture: Zeal for your house will devour me. The Jews intervened and said, "What sign can you show us to justify what you have done?" Jesus answered, "Destroy the sanctuary, and in three days I will raise it up." The Jews replied, "It has taken forty-six years to build this sanctuary: are you going to raise it up in three days?" But he was speaking of the sanctuary that was his body, and when Jesus rose from the dead, his disciples remembered that he had said this, and they believed the scripture and the words he had said.

During his stay in Jerusalem for the Passover many believed in his name when they saw the signs that he gave, but Jesus knew them all and did not trust himself to them; he never needed evidence about any man; he could tell what a man had in him.

John 2:13-25

NOT so long ago, a group of more than a hundred distinguished scholars issued a statement describing astrology

46

as a worthless fraud. For some reason these worthy gentle-
men thought that their scientific word would dissuade the
millions of people who take astrology seriously, or are at
least intrigued by its possibility. The professors should
have saved their time and energy. None of the enthusiasts
were daunted; indeed some of them even mounted picket
lines against the professors. Rational science is a poor
weapon with which to fight the human love for the marvelous, the miraculous. Signs and wonders practically
everybody wants.

The demand for scientific wonders plagued Jesus
throughout his life. It was not enough that he merely healed
the sick, and certainly not enough that he preached as no
one had ever preached before. His adversaries were not
content with a little bit of healing and a whole lot of wisdom; they wanted something spectacular. Turn off the sun
for a few days; produce an eclipse out of due season; make
the waters of the sea roll back, as Moses did; or, best of all,
call down ten plagues on the Roman invaders. If you do
that sort of thing, his adversaries said, then we'll take your
wisdom seriously, then we'll believe your preaching, then
we'll accept your good news, then we'll even acknowledge
your right to protest the corruption in the temple; but short
of something really spectacular, how can we be expected
to believe you?

Yahweh's warning through Moses to beware of signs and
wonders, the superstitious and the marvelous, clearly had
no effect on the adversaries of Jesus. Unfortunately the
immediate followers of Jesus were not immune from the
temptation either. The gospel writers, particularly Mark,
repeatedly had to warn their readers against the temptation to turn Jesus into a mere performer of marvels (an
especially skillful kind of magic-maker). Nor has the same
temptation been absent in the years since. Many Catholics

have an obsession with private revelations, unofficial miracles, terrifying prophecies and other strange, frightening, sensational phenomena. Some of us are old enough to remember the "bear will fight the eagle" prophecy that swept through Catholic colleges many years ago, causing terror among large numbers of people for several months. The gospel stories, teachings of Christian tradition, the sacraments and, more recently, the documents of the Vatican Council—these apparently are not enough. In fact, those who search after the marvelous, the miraculous consider what happened in a small town in Wisconsin, in a convent in the Philippines, or what happened to someone in a very private revelation to be the most important of all. Without realizing it, such Christians, sincere, perhaps, but misled, are demanding of Jesus the same signs and wonders as did the scribes and the Pharisees in John's gospel.

The sign Jesus offers is the sign of Jonah the prophet, the sign of someone buried in the earth. Jesus defies his enemies to destroy him, because no matter what they do to him, even if they bury him in a tomb, the heavenly Father will vindicate his preaching. In effect, Jesus is telling those who harass him that faith in God's love is far stronger, far more powerful, and far more important than the most spectacular miracle. What does he do to justify his anger at the corruption in the temple? He doesn't turn off the sun or push back the sea or get rid of the Romans; he cites his faith in God's love. That is the only sign he has, and that is the only sign he needs. If that sign is not good enough for others, and Jesus knows all too well that the most spectacular miracle will not change their minds, if a faith that is so powerful that it enables one to go bravely and confidently toward death on the cross does not persuade others, then nothing will persuade them.

In his famous poem, *The Ballad of the White Horse,*

G. K. Chesterton has the battered King Alfred hiding in the rushes along the river Thames. The Mother of God appears to him and the king pleads with the Blessed Mother for some sign or wonder that will pick up his faith and strengthen his resolve. But she will give him no sign. Such things, she says, are for infidels, pagans, magicians, and other superstitious unbelievers. They need such things to lighten their paths; but, she tells Alfred, those who are signed with the sign of the cross "go gaily in the dark." She gives him no encouragement at all: "I tell you naught for your comfort/ Yea, naught for your desire,/ Save that the sky grows darker yet/ And the sea rises higher." Far from trying to lift his spirits, Mary tells the Saxon king that things will get even worse, and just in case he is feeling too optimistic, she adds two more lines of gloom: "Night shall be thrice night over you,/ And heaven an iron cope." And then she offers him the same sign that Jesus threw in the face of his accusers in the temple precinct, "Do you have joy without a cause/ Yea, faith without a hope?"

In the face of all the grim and dreadful events that happened around Alfred in the poem and Jesus' followers in his time and after, is the sign of faith, the sign of the cross. It offers a cold, lonely, tenuous kind of hope, perhaps. No miracles, no wonders, no stars falling from heaven, no secret prophecies whispered in our ears, no hidden wisdom revealed to us by a soothsayer or a fortuneteller— just the cold, hard, rock-solid truth of faith. But what is it that faith tells us? Faith tells us that God loves us, and this is, if only we believe it, the greatest marvel, the most splendid miracle, the most spectacular wisdom that has ever existed. Christians can go gaily in the dark because they have been signed by the cross and already have a light within that no darkness can put out.

Together with Jesus we go up to Jerusalem during Lent for Good Friday. And we go up with fear and trembling, experiencing all the desolation that Jesus experienced in the garden and all the loneliness and frustration that every Christian from the time of Jesus (in this respect Alfred the Saxon king is every one of us) has experienced in life. But fear and anxiety do not put out the light of faith; what counts is not being immune from those feelings (which would only be true of angels) but continuing the journey despite our fear and anxiety. Faith does not eliminate terror, it does something much more wonderful: it enables us to go on despite terror.

12

The tax collectors and the sinners, meanwhile, were all seeking his company to hear what he had to say and the Pharisees and the scribes complained. "This man" they said "welcomes sinners and eats with them." So he spoke this parable to them:

He also said, "A man had two sons. The younger said to his father, 'Father, let me have the share of the estate that would come to me.' So the father divided the property between them. A few days later, the younger son got together everything he had and left for a distant country where he squandered his money on a life of debauchery.

"When he had spent it all, that country experienced a severe famine, and now he began to feel the pinch, so he hired himself out to one of the local inhabitants who put him on his farm to feed the pigs. And he would willingly have filled his belly with the husks the pigs were eating but no one offered him anything. Then he came to his senses and said, 'How many of my father's paid servants have more food than they want, and here am I dying of hunger! I will leave this place and go to my father and say: 'Father, I have sinned against heaven and against you; I no longer deserve to be called your son; treat me as one of your paid servants.' So he left the place and went back to his father.

"While he was still a long way off, his father saw him and was moved with pity. He ran to the boy, clasped him in his arms and kissed him tenderly. Then his son said, 'Father, I have sinned against heaven and against you. I no longer deserve to be called your son.' But the father said to his servants, 'Quick! Bring out the best robe and *put it on him; put a ring on his finger and sandals on his feet. Bring the calf we have been fattening, and kill it; we are going to have a feast, a celebration, because this son of mine was dead and has come back to life; he was lost and is found.' And they began to celebrate.*

"Now the elder son was out in the fields, and on his way back, as he drew near the house, he could hear music and dancing. Calling one of the servants he asked what it was all about. 'Your brother has come' replied the servant 'and your father has killed the calf we had fattened because he has got him back safe and sound.' He was angry then and refused to go in, and his father came out to plead with him; but he answered his father, 'Look, all these years I have slaved for you and never once disobeyed your orders, yet you never offered me so much as a kid for me to celebrate with my friends. But, for this son of yours, when he comes back after swallowing up your property—he and his women—you kill the calf we had been fattening.'

"The father said, 'My son, you are with me always and all I have is yours. But it was only right we should celebrate and rejoice, because your brother here was dead and has come to life; he was lost and is found.' "

Luke 15:1-3, 11-32

WHAT if the prodigal son were our kid? Can you imagine the stern lecture, the long, Polonius-like exhortation, the detailed warnings, the elaborate conditions we would put upon him before he could even begin to "earn his way back" (as some political leaders have said about "Vietnam deserters and draft-dodgers"). The young man had done a terrible thing. He had behaved irresponsibly despite our warnings; he ignored our superior wisdom, flauted our advice, ridiculed our knowledge; and now he comes crawling back. Well, good enough; we'll take him back only under the condition that he really show penitence, that he really crawl, that he really earn his way, every inch. And then, of course, when he is accepted back, he will have to be reminded often of how bad he was and how generous we were. By those standards, the father of the prodigal son was outrageously permissive, unconscionably lax; he had spoiled his son once and now the old fool was at it again.

We are accustomed to calling this parable "the prodigal son," but in fact it would be much more appropriately named the parable of "the loving father." There is no doubt at all that by human standards the father's behavior is bizarre, to say the least. The prodigal son hardly deserves admission back into the family, and it would not at all be unreasonable—on the contrary, it might be prudent —for the father to lay down stern conditions for reconciliation. Instead, he seems to have been waiting on the porch steps for the young man to appear on the road, rushes to meet him, cuts off the son's speech of apology, and promptly convenes a big party to celebrate. By our standards, such permissiveness would seem to be the surest way in the world to guarantee a repetition. We find ourselves wondering when the prodigal son will demand another cut of the inheritance to go off and waste it in gambling and vice a second time. We wonder how many more times he's going to be able to get away with it before his father finally clamps down.

The implications for our behavior are chilling. God has repeatedly made it clear that as he has forgiven us, so he expects us to forgive others; as he has been generous to us, so we must reflect the same generosity to him. He is not laying down patterns for disciplinary relationships between parents and children, though it is worth noting that by the standards of the society of Jesus' time, the behavior of the father was even more bizarre than such behavior would be considered in our time. Obviously there are some times in human relationships when parents must impose discipline on their children; the point of the parable is not that parental love should be without sanction but that parental love should be love, and that whenever it is necessary to impose sanctions, the generosity and love of the parent for the child should not be obscured, much less withdrawn. Love, the story of the prodigal son tells us, once given is given permanently and unconditionally; it is never used as a tool to manipulate, punish, control the one whom we love.

We have all had the experience of being generously forgiven. It is an extraordinarily good feeling. We have done wrong; we may have been mean, thoughtless, petty, cruel, insensitive, forgetful, clumsy, or just plain stupid. We don't deserve to be forgiven, we may even be afraid to ask to be forgiven; but the other person forgives us just the same, without strings attached, without punitive little digs, without animosity, without self-righteousness or self-congratulation. We are forgiven because we are loved; the slate is wiped clean, and we can start all over again. The peculiar thing about such forgiveness is that it enhances the personality and character of both the forgiver and the forgiven. Both become better human beings because they are caught up in such an exchange of loving generosity. The cause of the offense is indeed a kind of *felix culpa,* because out of it comes warmth, reconciliation, and love even stronger than that which existed before.

But while it is a marvelous experience to be spontaneously and generously forgiven, we are very reluctant to extend that forgiveness. We want to punish, we want to get our own pound of flesh, we want to get even, we want to force the other to apologize, we want the other to admit that he was wrong and we were right; we want to be vindicated, justified, triumphant. Besides, we are terribly afraid of the vulnerability that forgiveness induces; for if we forgive someone without punishment, without vengeance, without getting even, we leave ourselves open to being hurt once again. Such vulnerability doesn't seem to be worth the risk. It is good to be forgiven but risky to forgive.

The loving other often represents to us God's invitation to forgive, God's demand that we extend the same forgiveness to others that he has extended to us. But in any intimate relationship, spontaneous forgiveness is almost a medium of exchange. And if it is not spontaneous, generous, open, vulnerable without counting costs or getting even, the forgiveness simply won't be what it must be if the common life together is to be maintained. Forgiveness is not an option for the beloved, intimate other; forgiveness is a necessity. We must forgive the other; the other must be ready to forgive us in return. It is not an exchange the way we cash traveler's checks, but the way two people in love constantly manifest their love for one another by forgiving the mistakes, the errors, the insensitivities, the harshness that is part of any intimate human relationship.

The practical application of today's gospel is as disturbing as it is obvious. If God is willing to bestow such total, absurd forgiveness on us, then we must be ready to offer the same forgiveness to those whom we love. More than that, however, it is precisely because we live in the world created by such a benign and loving God—a God like the crazy father of the prodigal son—that we can have the confidence and the peace necessary to forgive others, particularly the other whom we love deeply.

13

Among those who went up to worship at the festival were some Greeks. These approached Philip, who came from Bethsaida in Galilee, and put this request to him, "Sir, we should like to see Jesus." Philip went to tell Andrew, and Andrew and Philip together went to tell Jesus.

Jesus replied to them:

"Now the hour has come
for the Son of Man to be glorified.
I tell you, most solemnly,
unless a wheat grain falls on the ground and dies,
it remains only a single grain;
but if it dies,
it yields a rich harvest.
Anyone who loves his life loses it;
anyone who hates his life in this world
will keep it for the eternal life.
If a man serves me, he must follow me,
wherever I am, my servant will be there too.
If anyone serves me, my Father will honor him.
Now my soul is troubled.
What shall I say:
Father, save me from this hour?
But it was for this very reason that I have come to this
   hour.
Father, glorify your name!"

A voice came from heaven, "I have glorified it, and I will glorify it again."

People standing by, who heard this, said it was a clap

*of thunder; others said, "It was an angel speaking to him."
Jesus answered, "It was not for my sake that this voice
came, but for yours. Now sentence is being passed on
this world; now the prince of this world is to be over-
thrown. And when I am lifted up from the earth, I shall
draw all men to myself."*

*By these words he indicated the kind of death he would
die.*

John 12:20-33

GIVING UP, surrendering, yielding, accepting—these are
some of the most painful experiences we can possibly have.
A parent must finally surrender a child to adulthood; the
dependent child must be given up, in order that he or she
might pursue an independent, mature life. A man and
woman in love with one another finally surrender to each
other; they give up the pretenses, the defenses, the subtle
manipulations by which both try to bend the other to fit a
particular plan. In the surrender that takes place—if it
does at all—the man and woman give each other the right
to "be," to be what they are in themselves and to accept
that which the other is. In terminal illness, the acceptance
of the reality of death is the absolutely essential prerequi-
site to adjusting to the finality of that reality. In all three
cases—raising children, falling in love, dying—we must
begin by giving up our own plans, our own ambitions, our
own needs, yielding to the implacable external reality—the
maturation of the child, the selfhood of the other, the inevitability of death. To yield to the implacability of the
reality beyond ourselves can be a terrifying experience
because it yields control, strips away defenses, puts us at
the mercy of the world outside.

Paradoxically enough, this surrender of the self—so frightening, so painful, so shattering—turns out to lead not to annihilation but to an opening up, to joy, peace and happiness—even ecstasy. When a parent finally lets a child become an adult, the parent may lose a dependent child but in the process gain an adult friend; and it is much better, much more satisfying, much more fulfilling when one of your offspring becomes an adult friend. Yielding to the selfhood of another in human sexual love, however shattering an experience it may be, means that you gain the other and enhance yourself. And surrendering to death, the death researchers tell us, leads not to terror but to peace, hope and, astonishingly, in the last minutes, to joy.

So John's gospel does not speak to an experience that is foreign to us but rather it emphasizes that Jesus also knew the terrors of surrender and the joys that come after it. After the Transfiguration experience on Mt. Tabor, he knew it was necessary to go up to Jerusalem to die; in this exchange with his apostles recounted here, occasioned by the visit of the Greeks, Jesus makes two critically important points. He explains both his own experience of the inevitability of death and the meaning of his own death for his followers. The grain of wheat has to die in order to produce much fruit; Jesus must surrender to his enemies and die in order that he might produce the fruit that is the church. So, too, all those who follow him. If they cling too desperately to their own fears, their own defenses, their own precious little life plans, they will lose their lives anyhow, because everyone must die; but if the followers of Jesus imitate him and bravely surrender to death with confidence in God's powerful love, they will gain eternal life. Jesus, by dying for love of us, draws all humanity to himself. If we live in such a way that the world sees we are unafraid of death, then we too will draw others to ourselves and, ultimately to Jesus.

The person who dies to what is often a lonely, defensive life, giving himself or herself over to the common life with a spouse must die to many old ways and habits. The lover who loves the "old" life will both lose the old life and never attain the new; but the one who bravely and cheerfully dies to the old selfish independence and merges selfhood with the reality of the common life, gains far more than what is lost. Like the grain of wheat, he or she has fallen to the earth and died, but will rise again to a richer, fuller, and more fruitful life. This is the nature of the human condition, this is the essence of human experience: We gain life by dying, we bear fruit by falling to the earth, we must be lifted up to draw all to ourselves. Death turns out not to be the end of life but the beginning. Each new experience of life that we permit ourselves is inevitably preceded by a surrender to some kind of death.

Jesus tells us how we should interpret his own suffering and death. He explains to us how we should live and die: We must surrender in order to possess, we must yield in order to grow, we must give up in order to obtain, we must die in order to live. Jesus died in order to show us how to die, and by so doing, he showed us also how to live—and thus he reinforced and validated for us that vague, persistent hunch that is built into the structure of our personalities and which tells us that no matter how strong death is, life is stronger. As G. K. Chesterton put it: "Life is too important ever to be anything else but life."

The gospel story is a preparation both for Good Friday and for Easter Sunday. It gives us the key to the meaning of surrender, it shows us how to prepare to die; but it also promises us that death does not have the final word. Baptism, which we renew on Easter morning, is both a death and a burial. We are submerged into the waters, but the waters are life-giving; so in baptism we die and rise again. Baptism commemorates both Good Friday and Easter; it is a sacrament which "stylizes" for us a life of surrender and conquest, of death and resurrection.

We often used to argue whether it was the whole life of Jesus that saved us or whether it was only his death. But in the light of this gospel, such a question is foolish. One can't separate the many deaths of a life from the final death. As the poet T. S. Eliot eloquently phrased it: "In my beginning is my end. . . . In my end is my beginning." As we live, so shall we die; death is not the end of life but the beginning of a new life, not a destruction but an accomplishment, an accomplishment which begins ritually when we die to the old self in baptism and continues throughout the rest of our lives. We surrender in order that we might live.

14

When evening came he arrived with the Twelve. And while they were at table eating, Jesus said, "I tell you solemnly, one of you is about to betray me, one of you eating with me." They were distressed and asked him, one after another, "Not I, surely?" He said to them, "It is one of the Twelve, one who is dipping into the same dish with me. Yes, the Son of Man is going to his fate, as the scriptures say he will, but alas for that man by whom the Son of Man is betrayed! Better for that man if he had never been born!"

And as they were eating he took some bread, and when he had said the blessing he broke it and gave it to them. "Take it," he said "this is my body." Then he took a cup, and when he had returned thanks he gave it to them, and all drank from it, and he said to them, "This is my blood, the blood of the covenant, which is to be poured out for many. I tell you solemnly, I shall not drink any more wine until the day I drink the new wine in the kingdom of God."

After psalms had been sung they left for the Mount of Olives. And Jesus said to them, "You will all lose faith, for the scripture says: I shall strike the shepherd and the sheep will be scattered, however after my resurrection I shall go before you to Galilee." Peter said, "Even if all lose faith, I will not." And Jesus said to him, "I tell you solemnly, this day, this very night, before the cock crows twice, you will have disowned me three times." But he repeated still more earnestly, "If I have to die with you, I will never disown you." And they all said the same.

Mark 14:17-31

WHILE the gospel accounts of the suffering and death of Jesus are distinct narrations, Mark's gospel appears to combine two earlier versions of the crucifixion. The first and more ancient of the two is to be found in Mark 15:20, 22,24 and 27, and shows a good deal of implicit reference to both Psalm 22 and Isaiah 53. In this Passion story, one can detect an early apologetic attempt. How could it possibly be, early Christians and their friends and neighbors asked, that someone as wonderful as the Christians claim Jesus was, should suffer such a horrible death? The response was that Jesus was to be identified with the righteous servant of God, the suffering servant of the prophet Isaiah. Accordingly, one serves God by bravely accepting the sufferings of life.

The later tradition is to be found in Mark 15:25,26,29, 32,34,37,38, and turns from an apologetic interpretation of the suffering to an eschatological one. There is a war in heaven, a struggle between good and evil, between life and death, between darkness and light. The outcry of Jesus at the end is an announcement of the triumph of light over darkness, of good over evil, of life over death. Thus there is in the crucifixion story both an ethical, or apologetic, interpretation and a cosmic, or eschatological, interpretation. Jesus is indeed the suffering servant but also, in the words of Irenaeus, the *Christus victor*. The key point, made over and over during Holy Week, is that Christ became the victor precisely by being the suffering servant, and that we too become victors insofar as we are capable of being suffering servants.

The idea of service is echoed once again in the Holy Thursday liturgy. Jesus serves his apostles by washing their feet, and then makes himself available for the service of all humankind through the institution of the Eucharist and through the establishment of his priesthood, and finally by issuing the instruction that all Christians are to love one another as Jesus has loved them. Jesus serves his brethren as his brethren are to serve one another and all humankind. The Eucharist and the priesthood link the service Jesus rendered to the service we are all to render.

Many contemporary writers think that the "last" supper may not have been the formal Passover dinner but merely a typical Jewish ritual meal among a group of friends. Others think that it was a kind of anticipated Passover which Jesus ate a day early because he knew he would be dead on the morrow. Still others think that there were different calendars being used by different groups within the Jewish community. The important point to remember, however, is that the Passover, while it was the epitome and the apex of Jewish ritual meals, was by no means the only ritual meal. Each family dinner was something of a ritual, and each family dinner was supposed to contain some sort of "eucharist," that is a prayer of thanksgiving for God's blessings. Jesus and his followers had eaten many such meals together in their lives, meals which both celebrated and reinforced the bonds of love, friendship, and unity which held them together. Their final meal together, then, while it was certainly different from the preceding ones, did not come as a surprise; it was not discontinuous with the custom of giving thanks to God and celebrating the Eucharist at each of their common meals. The transition from the Last Supper to the Eucharistic ceremonies of the early church, then, would have been easy and natural. But we must ask ourselves today whether the way we celebrate the Eucharist gives much evidence that we perceive it as a meal in which we celebrate and give thanks.

The fifty-third chapter of the prophet Isaiah keeps returning explicitly and implicitly throughout Holy Week. There is considerable debate among scripture scholars whether Jesus himself identified with the suffering servant of Isaiah, or whether the identification was made later by the early Christians, seeking in the repertory of religious symbols and imagery available to them to articulate and describe the experiences they had of the Jesus who had died and risen.

This debate about the suffering servant imagery is interesting, but it is not particularly important save for the fact that it emphasizes for us how religious language comes to be used. The early Christians had an experience of a Jesus who died and lived again. It was a powerful, vivid, overwhelming experience. He was an innocent person who willingly and bravely—though not without fear—went to his own death because of his absolute conviction that God's loving power would validate the Good News he had preached; and sure enough, God did validate that Good News by disclosing Jesus to his followers as gloriously and supremely alive. But how to describe the bravery, courage, generosity, and fidelity with which Jesus went to his death? The early Christian preachers and writers easily and naturally turned to the prophet Isaiah, perhaps because Jesus himself used the language of Isaiah or simply because it was so appropriate. Merit comes not from merely suffering but by being a suffering *servant,* one who bravely, confidently, lovingly accepts the crosses of life and thus bears witness to one's faith in a loving God who will overcome all the crosses and the suffering.

The early Christians, like all of us, had experienced the isolation, the alienation, the loneliness, the fear, the sluggishness, the anxiety that are part of the human condition. They experienced the need to be reconciled and the need to be free. Then in Jesus they understood that they had received both reconciliation and freedom; they had been redeemed and liberated. Jesus had "purchased" their freedom, he had "paid their debts." While the theological issues of salvation and atonement are complex ones, it would be a serious mistake during Holy Week to dwell too long on those complexities and overlook the fundamental religious facts: Whatever theological interpretations and explanations the early Christians, or we ourselves, may choose to use, what we are talking about are fundamental experiences of freedom and unity, of liberation and reconciliation.

15

It was very early on the first day of the week and still dark, when Mary of Magdala came to the tomb. She saw that the stone had been moved away from the tomb and came running to Simon Peter and the other disciple, the one Jesus loved. "They have taken the Lord out of the tomb" she said "and we don't know where they have put him."

So Peter set out with the other disciple to go to the tomb. They ran together, but the other disciple, running faster than Peter, reached the tomb first; he bent down and saw the linen cloths lying on the ground, but did not go in. Simon Peter who was following now came up, went right into the tomb, saw the linen cloths on the ground, and also the cloth that had been over his head; this was not with the linen cloths but rolled up in a place by itself. Then the other disciple who had reached the tomb first also went in; he saw and he believed. Till this moment they had failed to understand the teaching of scripture, that he must rise from the dead.

John 20:1-9

WE can only appreciate the meaning of Easter if we understand that it is a *spring* feast. Not long ago a very distinguished theologian wrote an article in which he said he was disgusted with all the pagan references to spring he heard in Easter Sunday sermons. In the southern hemisphere, South America and particularly Africa, where that distinguished theologian said the future of the church lies, it is not spring at all during Easter. In the years to come, he rejoiced, when the church will be a southern hemisphere church, the link between Easter and spring will be broken. The Resurrection of the Lord will no longer be seen as a pagan festival celebrating the rebirth of nature. The distinguished theologian was terribly upset by all the pagan and Jewish symbols which had been taken over by Christians (and he suggested that Jews were also upset by such pilfering of their symbols). The feast of the Resurrection of Jesus ought to be purified, in his opinion, from all such "borrowed" imagery.

A long time ago, when some of us were quite young, there was a popular song called, "It Might As Well Be Spring." The early Christians who poured spring imagery into their celebration of the Resurrection were not trying to write geography or climatology; they were not meteorologists trying to provide a forecast for the Easter parade; they were not saying that Easter would have no meaning if it should rain or snow on that day. If we went to the early Christians and said, "Look, it's not spring where we live," they would hardly have known what to say in response. They probably would have said something like, "But you know what spring is like, don't you?" For that was all they tried to do when they linked the feast of the Resurrection to the Jewish season of Passover. They wanted us to think of spring even if it did not happen to be spring. Easter is not spring and spring is not Easter, but they are both linked to a deeper, richer and more powerful reality so that spring helps to explain the feast of the Resurrection of the Lord and the feast of the Resurrection in its turn gives us deeper and richer insight into what spring means.

And that ultimate reality of spring is simply rebirth. The sun rises in the morning after it has set the night before; we get out of bed (sometimes, anyhow) refreshed; we get over most of our sicknesses and experience the rebirth of physical health; we come alive again after anguish, grief, and quarrel; rain finally falls on the fields to end the drought; winter ends, whether it be the benign season in California or the dread ones of northern Minnesota; and the life of nature, dead for many months, reasserts itself. Brown turns to green, gray to blue, darkness turns to light. Rebirth seems to be a given in both the human condition and in the physical universe. The critical question is not whether the rebirth of Jesus can be linked with the rebirth of spring, but whether rebirth ought to be taken seriously at all. Is life really birth? Does death really lead to rebirth? Is life really the preparation for resurrection that it often seems to be?

The Resurrection of Jesus confirms and validates this hunch, this hope, this expectation of ours. It says yes, indeed, life is a preparation for death, but death is a transition between life and resurrection. Jesus lived in order that he might die; but he died in order that he might live; and he lives in order that we might all live. Life is rebirth, life is a resurrection. The Resurrection of Jesus is not so much "proof" in the sense that we prove a mathematical theorem; it is a validation of our suspicion, a confirmation of our hunch, a reinforcement of our hope, a reassurance of our dreams. We can afford to rejoice at Easter not merely because Jesus has risen but because we see in the Resurrection of Jesus a confirmation of our dim and faint hopes for resurrection. At Eastertime we celebrate our own resurrections, we celebrate our now profound and powerful conviction that human existence, for all its elements of winter —cold and bitter death, disappointment and frustration— is in the final analysis a spring experience, an experience of hope, rebirth, joy, new life.

So the early Christians saw no reason why they should not continue the Jewish Passover ceremony, a spring ritual which celebrated the new life of freedom of the children of Israel and merged the pre-Sinai fertility feasts of the Paschal Lamb and the Unleavened Bread. Fertility and the new life now came not from the powers of nature but from Yahweh, the One Who Gave Life and would give it again. It was the same Yahweh that both Christians and Jews believed in; it was the same renewing, reassuring, renovating Yahweh; and it was the same new life that was to be celebrated, a new life in which now the Christians perceived even greater meaning than their predecessors had, because there was now not only a renewing Yahweh in whom they believed but a Yahweh who promised resurrection. Why not celebrate the Resurrection of Jesus at springtime? And if it doesn't happen to be spring where you are, well, it is still a time of new life in the Resurrection of Jesus, a rebirth that is not an imitation of spring but rather a rebirth of which spring is merely a hint. The Resurrection of Jesus, the church tells us today, is like spring only better.

Christmas and Easter are really the same feast. Christmas is a feast of birth, Easter a feast of rebirth. Both are feasts of fresh, clean, new starts. When Jesus came into the world, humankind was renewed; it began all over again in a sense. With the resurrection, that renewal was brought to its fulfillment. Christmas reminds us through the birth of a child of our experiences of renewal; Easter reminds us of renewal by talking about spring. But in both cases the emphasis is on newness, freshness, starting again, having a second chance, being reborn. Both feasts tell us that life is stronger than death. This is the only reason we celebrate at Easter and the only reason why we celebrate at Christmas. Life is stronger than death. Indeed, every feast in the Christian calendar is a celebration of the triumph of life over death.

16

In the evening of that same day, the first day of the week, the doors were closed in the room where the disciples were, for fear of the Jews. Jesus came and stood among them. He said to them, "Peace be with you," and showed them his hands and his side. The disciples were filled with joy when they saw the Lord, and he said to them again, "Peace be with you. As the Father sent me, so am I sending you." After saying this he breathed on them and said:

> *"Receive the Holy Spirit,*
> *For those whose sins you forgive,*
> *they are forgiven;*
> *for those whose sins you retain,*
> *they are retained."*

Thomas, called the Twin, who was one of the Twelve, was not with them when Jesus came. When the disciples said, "We have seen the Lord," he answered, "Unless I see the holes that the nails made in his hands and can put my finger into the holes they made, and unless I can put my hand into his side, I refuse to believe." Eight days later the disciples were in the house again and Thomas was with them. The doors were closed, but Jesus came in and stood among them. "Peace be with you" he said. Then he spoke to Thomas, "Put your finger here; look, here are my hands. Give me your hand; put it into my side. Doubt no longer but believe." Thomas replied, "My Lord and my God!" Jesus said to him: "You believe because you can see me. Happy are those who have not seen and yet believe."

There were many other signs that Jesus worked and the

disciples saw, but they are not recorded in this book. These are recorded so that you may believe that Jesus is the Christ, the Son of God, and that believing this you may have life through his name .

John 20:19-31

WE have all known moments of doubt, hesitation, uncertainty. Should we quit our job and try a new one? Should we marry or not? Should we move to a new house? How should we discipline an unruly child? How to answer the same child's baffled questions? Sometimes in our uncertainty we have a pretty good idea of what we ought to do, but we are not sure whether we are strong enough to do it. At other times our hesitation is brought on by a complete lack of information. We have to do something; we have to decide, but the arguments pro and con seem to cancel each other out. What to do, what to do?

To believe or not to believe; that was the question that faced the doubting Thomas. The others told him that the Lord had risen, that he had brought peace and even the promise of the forgiveness of sins. Thomas was not, after all, a complete fool. He might have been the butt of jokes of the more quick-minded others, but he was certainly smart enough to know that they would not be "pulling his leg" about a matter so grave as this. It was hard to believe that the master had risen, but they all seemed to believe it. What was even worse, however, was believing the implications of that Resurrection; for the master, in his earliest apparitions to the apostles had spoken of peace and the power to forgive sins. If men went around claiming to exercise the power to forgive sins, they would certainly be in trouble; they would need all the "peace" they could get

71

to survive the suffering, the misunderstanding, the criticism the animosity that they were bound to encounter. Thomas was not altogether sure that he wanted to be persuaded that the Lord had risen.

He did not have much choice in the matter, as it turned out. For there, in the midst of them, a week later was the Lord himself to back up the claims of Thomas' fellow apostles. He came to offer solace and peace to them all, as well as the power to forgive, which was a consequent of the former; for unless the peace of Jesus was within you, you could not forgive others even as he did. Thomas went along with the deal, but it is important for us to note that he did not have to. Like the others, he could have said no. The story of Thomas was written down primarily for those early Christians who felt discriminated against. There were people still alive who had known Jesus personally (though by the time of this gospel, there could have been only a few of them left). The gospel makes clear that just being in personal contact with Jesus wasn't enough. Thomas knew him through his whole public life, and he had the solemn word of all his friends that Jesus had risen. Still he was afraid of the terrifying implications of the Resurrection and was only won over when Jesus was there to invite him to touch the wounds. And as Jesus quickly noted, it wasn't the seeing that counted, it was the believing; one could believe without having seen.

The first-century complainers and all of us who have come after are thereby served due notice that in religious matters seeing really isn't believing. You can see and not necessarily believe—as did many others who knew Jesus— and you can believe without having seen. Belief is a cold, lonely leap in the dark. It was for Peter and James and John, it was for Thomas, it was for first-Century Christians, and it is for us today.

It is the message of joy, goodness, hope, love, life that is contained in the Easter experience of the early Christians. Indeed, it is the revelation of what human life means. The evidence is finally inconclusive; the arguments pro and con can ultimately persuade us that it is not irrational to believe, but they cannot make us believe. Indeed, it is only after we take the blind leap of faith and experience the evidence of living the Christian life that the arguments become absolutely conclusive. Thomas did not believe because he had touched the wounds of Jesus; having already believed, the experience of touching Jesus strengthened his faith.

We like to think of faith, when we talk about it, as a single act, a single leap. One makes up one's mind on a given day that one will be a Christian, makes an act of faith, and that's that. Or it seems to be that way in the old catechism books and theology manuals. In fact, though, we know from the experience of our daily life that doubt and uncertainty are religious problems that are constantly with us, and the leap of faith must be renewed often in life. To renew a decision is not to throw the decision itself into question, any more than the renewal of the Easter promises or the renewal of the marriage vows on wedding anniversaries can in any sense be said to question the original commitment. Renewal of a commitment looks forward to its continuation, not backward to its inception. It looks forward to new circumstances with new problems, new challenges, and new opportunities. We make repeated leaps of faith in our life, not because we doubt a previous one but because now we find ourselves in conditions and circumstances which demand that we leap again. It gets easier with practice, but it is never really easy to say with Thomas, "My Lord and my God." It takes strength and courage because it means, as Thomas well knew, that we embrace an aspect of Christ that gives us the power to forgive and guarantees us a life of both joy and suffering, or resurrection and the cross.

The link between faith and forgiveness in John's gospel is an important one. One can only give forgiveness and one can only receive it if first one believes in the life of the risen Jesus. Unless you have hope in your own resurrection, you will be too frightened to forgive and too terrified of the demand for conversion and transformation that the acceptance of forgiveness imposes. If the "firm purpose of amendment" after our confessions was so often ineffective, part of the reason may well be that we did not have a strong enough faith to believe that we really have been forgiven and are now really free to transform our lives.

17

That very same day, two of them were on their way to a village called Emmaus, seven miles from Jerusalem, and they were talking together about all that had happened. Now as they talked this over, Jesus himself came up and walked by their side; but something prevented them from recognizing him. He said to them, "What matters are you discussing as you walk along?" They stopped short, their faces downcast.

Then one of them, called Cleopas, answered him, "You must be the only person staying in Jerusalem who does not know the things that have been happening there these last few days." "What things?" he asked. "All about Jesus of Nazareth" they answered "who proved he was a great prophet by the things he said and did in the sight of God and of the whole people; and how our chief priests and our leaders handed him over to be sentenced to death, and had him crucified. Our own hope had been that he would be the one to set Israel free. And this is not all: two whole days have gone by since it all happened, and some women from our group have astounded us: they went to the tomb in the early morning, and when they did not find the body, they came back to tell us they had seen a vision of angels who declared he was alive. Some of our friends went to the tomb and found everything exactly as the women had reported, but of him they saw nothing."

Then he said to them, "You foolish men! So slow to believe the full message of the prophets! Was it not ordained that the Christ should suffer and so enter into his glory?" Then, starting with Moses and going through all the prophets, he explained to them the passages throughout the scriptures that were about himself.

*When they drew near to the village to which they were
going, he made as if to go on; but they pressed him to stay
with them. "It is nearly evening" they said "and the day
is almost over." So he went in to stay with them. Now
while he was with them at table, he took the bread and
said the blessing; then he broke it and handed it to them.
And their eyes were opened and they recognized him; but
he had vanished from their sight. Then they said to each
other, "Did not our hearts burn within us as he talked to
us on the road and explained the scriptures to us?"*

*They set out that instant and returned to Jerusalem.
There they found the Eleven assembled together with their
companions, who said to them, "Yes it is true. The Lord
has risen and has appeared to Simon." Then they told their
story of what had happened on the road and how they
had recognized him at the breaking of bread.*

Luke 24:13-25

ALBERT CAMUS, the French existentialist writer, was a
lonely and melancholy man. More aware than most of us
about the loneliness and misery of human life, he wrote
some beautiful lines about friendship. They are appropriate
words for every community, particularly a community of
friends, and especially for that community of friends we
call the church. "Don't walk in front of me, I may not
follow; don't walk behind me, I may not lead. Walk beside me and just be my friend." It's worth wondering
whether in Camus' unconscious there was a recollection
of the Emmaus story from the gospel in which Jesus is
neither in front of his friends nor behind them but rather
walking beside them, ready even to sit next to them at
supper.

Why do we have birthday parties, anniversary dinners, wedding banquets, graduation parties? Why do humans choose to celebrate major turning points in their lives with a meal? Why, in particular, do husband and wife go out to dinner on their wedding anniversary? What is there about eating together on that day which celebrates, re-affirms, strengthens love and recommits it to the challenges and the opportunities that still remain? What is there about a common meal that is so rich in meaning?

We know that many of our family meals are anything but peaceful. Think of the family dinner in the popular movie *Saturday Night Fever,* for example, in which husband and wife and children snarled and snapped at one another and even physically assaulted one another almost as a matter of daily routine. Most of our family meals are not that bad, but we do know that intimate family meals can often be anything but pleasant. Eating with the family becomes really important to us when we haven't done it for a long time. Then we realize that despite the conflicts and the troubles, it is desperately important to be together around the table with those we love, and how terrible it is to have to eat alone.

Eating is essential for life; it keeps us alive. So, too, is love essential for life. Love is to the soul what food is to the body. In an intimate meal between friends and lovers, body and soul combine; the body feeds on meat and drink, the soul on love. In the relaxed, affectionate, intimate at-mosphere that, at least in its best moments, the family meal provides, our love deepens, grows, becomes rich and powerful, and gives new direction and purpose to our lives.

The intimate meal, then, symbolizes loving communion, celebrates it, confirms it. Jesus and his followers had many such meals in the course of their life together, meals that strengthened and deepened the bonds of affection and

77

friendship which held them together—relaxed, informal, casual meals in which they came to know one another and, of course, came to know him. The Eucharist at the Last Supper was only the last of these meals they had together. Because it was the last, it took on special significance and became a sacrament. We continue it as a sacrament today precisely for the same reason that husbands and wives go off together on their wedding anniversary. One could even say that each mass is a wedding anniversary meal celebrating the marriage union between Jesus and his church. It strengthens the vitality of our union with Jesus and with one another.

The church tells us through the liturgy during the Easter season that it is through the Eucharist that the love of God revealed to us in Jesus at the resurrection is strengthened, continued, celebrated, renewed. Easter is the life of the church; the Eucharist makes Easter present every day.

It is essential for us to remember that the mass and Holy Communion were meant to be an intimate meal among friends, like the Last Supper, like the breaking of bread between Jesus and his disciples at Emmaus, like an anniversary dinner for a husband and wife. Our liturgies don't always seem like that; sometimes they can't. But we should still strive to understand that we are most especially a church, most especially a community of friends and lovers, when we have come together to sit around the banquet table of the Lord. After each Eucharist we must go back into the world outside and live lives as filled with love as that of husband and wife leaving a restaurant after an anniversary dinner together.

18

"I tell you most solemnly, anyone who does not enter the sheepfold through the gate, but gets in some other way is a thief and a brigand. The one who enters through the gate is the shepherd of the flock; the gatekeeper lets him in, the sheep hear his voice, one by one he calls his own sheep and leads them out. When he has brought out his flock, he goes ahead of them, and the sheep follow because they knew his voice. They never follow a stranger but run away from him: they do not recognize the voice of strangers."

Jesus told them this parable but they failed to understand what he meant by telling it to them.

So Jesus spoke to them again:

"I tell you most solemnly,
I am the gate of the sheepfold.
All others who have come
are thieves and brigands;
but the sheep took no notice of them.
I am the gate.
Anyone who enters through me will be safe:
he will go freely in and out
and be sure of finding pasture.
The thief comes
only to steal and kill and destroy.
I have come
so that they may have life
and have it to the full."

John 10:1-10

IN every close human relationship there is conflict, failure, disappointment, tension, strain, personality differences which separate even the most committed of lovers, threatening to tear the relationship apart or even destroy it. But then, after conflict, there come sorrow, regret, apology, reconciliation, and greater love. Our human love grows not by avoiding conflict and failure but by becoming richer and deeper because of our ability to transcend conflict and failure. In the story of the Good Shepherd we learn that Jesus is the gate of the sheepfold, and through him we can enter and then re-enter the community of his followers, if only we are ready to try to transform our lives and begin again.

If we have had any experience at all with love or with deep friendship, we know that the secret of intimacy is reconciliation. None of us is so skilled or so loving as to be able to avoid hurting the one we love, weakening the bonds that link us together, even threatening to rupture the fabric of our affection. Experienced lovers quickly learn that the secret is not so much to avoid conflict as to become good at reconciliation. Reconciliation isn't easy; it involves sorrow and a determination to begin again, to transform one's life with full awareness, of course, that the transformation will be incomplete and imperfect and that at some later time (the next hour, the next day, the next week), we will have to go through another transformation and begin still once again.

Usually the image we have of the Good Shepherd is of his going forth to hunt for the lost sheep in the mountains and in the valleys. Today's image is a little different, though it conveys the same message. Today Jesus is the gate through which the faithful come and go, venturing forth in the morning into the pastures in order that they might find their daily food and returning in the evening to the peace and security of the sheepfold (something like a corral) where they will be secure from the dangers that lurk in the night. Jesus, in other words, is the way into the church and the way out of the church when we go forth into the world to live the lives of Christians. Jesus attracts us into the church with the excitement and promise of his message, and then, having won us over by his love, sends us forth into the world to tell others about the excitement and love. Jesus, who showed us by his life and death how much God loves us, also shows us how the members of the community of his friends should live—by loving other human beings the way he loves us.

Our love affair with God in the sheepfold of Jesus is like all love affairs in which fragile, inadequate human beings become involved. Mistakes, conflicts, and reconciliation are as much a part of it as breathing is to human life.

"Metanoia," transformation, a profound change in the way we live, is not something that happens once, for all; it is something which we have to begin over and over again. We are not perfect, we are nowhere near perfect; we blunder and bungle, quit and cheat, evade and dissemble, fake and hedge, and then often fall flat on our faces. But still the sheepfold is open and Jesus stands at the gate telling us to come back in. It is never too late to start again, never too late to renew the transformation, never too late to repent, recommit ourselves to our baptismal promises. The only unforgivable sin, the smiling Jesus tells us at the gate, is not to come back and try again.

The story of the Good Shepherd should always be profoundly encouraging for us. It reveals how much God loves us, how ready he is to forgive, how easy it is to begin again. Today we ask ourselves what kind of metanoia, what kind of transformation, must happen to us. When the sun sets and it is time to go back to the sheepfold, will we say to the smiling Jesus at the gate, "Let's try once again." There is, of course, no better way to be reconciled with Jesus than to be reconciled to those whom we must love in this world.

19

"I am the true vine,
and my Father is the vinedresser.
Every branch in me that bears no fruit
he cuts away,
and every branch that does bear fruit he prunes
to make it bear even more.
You are pruned already,
by means of the word that I have spoken to you.
Make your home in me, as I make mine in you.
As a branch cannot bear fruit all by itself,
but must remain part of the vine,
neither can you unless you remain in me.
I am the vine,
you are the branches.
Whoever remains in me, with me in him,
bears fruit in plenty;
for cut off from me you can do nothing.
Anyone who does not remain in me
is like a branch that has been thrown away
—he withers;
these branches are collected and thrown on the fire,
and they are burned.
If you remain in me
and my words remain in you,
you may ask what you will
and you shall get it.
It is to the glory of my Father that you should bear
*   much fruit,*
and then you will be my disciples."

John 15:1-8

THE Welsh poet Dylan Thomas advised us not to go "gentle into that good night" but urges us to "rage, rage against the dying of the light." Don't accept life's trials and sufferings passively but raise Cain about them. And above all, Thomas said, do not acquiesce passively to the ultimate snuffing out of life that is our death. It is intolerable that our lives should be taken away from us. What a strange, bizarre universe it is that produces a creature who among all the others is the only one who can reflect upon its own death, a creature with a hunger for life that never ends, as well as the certain knowledge that life will end. It is not fair; the light should never go out.

But life is not fair. No one ever seriously argued that it was. The good suffer and the evil prosper complained the author of the Psalms. Our hopes are blighted, our dreams turn into nightmares, our expectations never seem to be realized, our plans don't work out right, it rains on our parade and all human activities, given half a chance, go wrong. We're subject to sinus infections, nervous stomachs, migrane headaches, jet lag, motion sickness, discouragement, disillusionment, frustration, and aging. The old prayer about life being a "vale of tears" isn't said anymore at the end of Mass, but despite all the postconciliar optimism, the world has not become a noticeably better place. Suffering is the lot of all humankind. Some of us die young, the rest of us grow old and die; but we all die, and it doesn't seem fair. Why should we be born into the world only to die?

Yet there are times when all the senseless suffering does not seem in vain. A mother suffers to bring a child into the world, but she rejoices when it is born. There should be, it seems to us, less painful ways to give birth; but we are still glad that birth can be given. Our personality grows, develops, becomes richer, more mature, more sensitive mostly through the painful and difficult process of learning by our mistakes. There ought to be some better way of learning, but we are still glad that we can learn. Love normally grows deeper and richer through reconciliation after quarrels. It would be far more pleasant, of course, if growth in love could be done some other way than through reconciliation after conflict, but we are glad that reconciliation is always a possibility. Human friendships which will last the rest of our lives are forged in difficult, dangerous situations. There ought to be easier ways of forming intimate friendships than shared adversity; King Hal and his followers paid a heavy price for becoming a "band of brothers" on St. Crispin's Day. But we are glad that it is possible to have deep, strong, and enduring friendships with our fellow human beings. The sufferings of childbirth, reconciliation, learning through trial and error, and facing adversity together still don't seem fair, but we are occasionally able to glimpse through them the silver lining of the dark, dismal clouds of life.

Jesus did not come into the world to try to explain to us the unfairness of life. He did not endeavor to give us a satisfactory rationale for the phenomenon of human suffering. He did not say that if we listened to him we would understand the great mysteries of evil, suffering and death that have such a clammy grip on human existence. Jesus came to tell us that God loves us and that his love is stronger than evil, suffering and death. He came to affirm that often very faint hope we have that in the long run, when the last word is said, life will turn out to be fair after all, and that we will ultimately and finally understand the why of suffering. And we perceive that from God's perspective the crooked lines do indeed look straight.

The parables of Jesus are filled with paradoxes, seeming contradictions which illustrate the truth of God's love. The vinedresser loves the vine; he expends tremendous energy in planting it, cultivating it, bringing it to fruit. But paradoxically he also trims the vine, cuts it, hurts it, permits it to suffer so that it might become stronger and bear better and richer fruit. We trim our rose bushes not because we hate the rose bush, but because we love the roses that the pruned bush will produce more abundantly. Yet from the bush's viewpoint, the pruning is decidedly unfair.

The parable of the vine and the branches is not meant to be an explanation of the "problem of suffering"; it would not admit of precise and logical metaphysical analysis. It is at the most a hint of an explanation, a shaft of blinding light breaking the darkness for but a moment. The parable tells us that God loves us and that life results from his love even though it may seem unfair. But after that quick flash of light, there is darkness once again. However, when we stop to think about it for a moment, we understand what we saw in that brief moment of illumination. Those who bear the unfairness and the suffering of life with faith, confidence and courage, hopefulness and generosity, without complaint or recrimination and without imposing their own suffering on others do indeed become richer, better, fuller, more authentic human beings. One dies on one's own cross in order that one might rise on one's own Easter.

In the original Old Testament imagery, the vine was Israel; in the New Testament, it sometimes means the church and it sometimes means the individual Christian. In John's gospel, the imagery is that the vine is the whole church, with Jesus the stem and the individual Christians the branches. The pruning can stand for either the elimination of unproductive branches or the trimming of productive branches so that they will bear even more fruit. Note well that these productive branches are sustained in life despite the trauma of pruning precisely because they are united with Jesus. The point is that we are best able to suffer the heartaches, the unfairness, the injustice, the indignities, the frustrations of life if we are united with Jesus. In our union with the crucified and risen Lord, in other words, we acquire the hope and the confidence we need to see our way through our own crucifixion to our own eventual resurrection.

20

"If anyone loves me he will keep my word,
and my Father will love him,
and we shall come to him
and make our home with him.
Those who do not love me do not keep my words.
And my word is not my own:
it is the word of the one who sent me.
I have said these things to you
while still with you;
but the Advocate, the Holy Spirit,
whom the Father will send in my name,
will teach you everything
and remind you of all I have said to you.
Peace I bequeath to you,
my own peace I give you,
a peace the world cannot give, this is my gift to you.
Do not let your hearts be troubled or afraid.
You heard me say:
I am going away, and shall return.
If you loved me you would have been glad to know
*   that I am going to the Father,*
for the Father is greater than I.
I have told you this now before it happens,
so that when it does happen you may believe."

John 14:23-29

ONE of the toughest things in life is making decisions—
where to go to school, what kind of a job to get, who to

marry, where to live, whether to move, whether to change jobs. All of these things require an aye or nay; we cannot stay home *and* go away; we cannot go south *and* north too. Indeed, the more complicated our lives get the more decisions we have to make, and each generation seems to have even more decisions to face than its predecessors. Decision-making is difficult precisely because we can never be certain about the outcome. We can calculate the odds, estimate the probabilities, gather computer print-outs to tell us what our chances are; but in the final analysis every decision requires some kind of risks. If there were no risks, there would be no need for a decision. Some of us try to hedge, try to get through life without making decisions, responding always to external pressures by yielding to whichever are the strongest. The nice thing about that strategy is that we can always blame some force outside ourselves when we've made a mistake. The bad thing about it is that we then lead lives devoid of personal responsibility.

Life requires many leaps in the dark, many acts of almost blind trust, many risks that have been calculated carefully but are still risky. Following our instincts "playing it by ear," is part of the human condition whether we like it or not. Still there are times when we *know* that however uncertain the odds, however imponderable the eventuality, however unpredictable the outcome, we simply know that there is something we should do—go to this school, choose that career, marry this person. We do not ignore rational calculations but go beyond their limits and take the leap of faith, a leap which seems blind but which we know in our hearts is the leap to take.

We must very carefully understand what happens in such decisive acts. We may say that we "feel" what we should do, or that our "instincts" tell us what we should do, that we have a "hunch" that it will work out all right. In fact, what we usually mean is that we are using certain styles of knowing that go beyond rationality and combine all the resources of personality—instincts, emotion, will, subconscious and unconscious. They all combine to tell us that this particular decision responds to that which is best, most generous, most outgoing, and most authentic in ourselves. Marry this man or woman? The odds are that it would be a good thing, but in the depths of our personality we also *know* beyond any calculation that this is indeed a person we should marry.

It is precisely to that sharp, refined, deep part of our personality that the Holy Spirit speaks. Paul tells us that God's Spirit speaks to our spirit. He means that the Paraclete, the one who Jesus promised in this gospel is God inviting, calling forth that which is most noble, most authentic, most appealing, most generous in us. It is to our "hunch," "instinct," and "feel" that the Spirit appeals; he does not deny rationality, of course, and he assumes that rationality is at work. The Paraclete goes beyond rationality, however, and appeals to that which is most authentic in the total human person that is each one of us. God's Spirit, in other words, usually works on us quite indirectly, speaking to us, appealing to us, inviting us, calling us forth in and through the people and opportunities that daily come our way.

The Paraclete, then, does not come down and whisper in our ear—though sometimes the power of his call is so strong that it is almost as though there is a voice telling us what to do. We *know* which decision is most authentically us, and we know, if we stop to think about it, that the Spirit is calling.

Our instincts can be wrong, of course, our hunches inaccurate, our "feel" self-deceptive. This supra-irrational way of knowing is by no means infallible. We may think the Paraclete is inviting us when in fact it is a "false" Spirit (which does not necessarily or ordinarily imply demonic activity—it only implies a mistake). One of the reasons for having a community of friends—we call it the church —is that it can help us discern the Spirit and help us distinguish between the true and false spirits. That community can listen with us; and, knowing us better sometimes than we know ourselves, our friends can tell us, "You know, you're really kidding yourself," or, "Yeah, that does seem to be the right thing for you." And internally in our personalities, the Paraclete is a Spirit of peace. It is not the peace of absolute tranquility but that of challenge and excitement. If that to which we seem to be called by the Paraclete brings us greater peace with ourselves, our family, and our friends, makes us more open and loving and generous to those with whom we come in contact, then it is very likely the true Paraclete and not the false Spirit who is talking to us.

Christians have known for a long time that the Spirit speaks to us through others, going above and beyond the ordinary calculations of rationality. For centuries our predecessors evolved "rules" that showed remarkable insight into the human psychology and the human propensity for self-deception. In our era we seem to have lost a sense of the Holy Spirit and understanding of the need to discern the operations of the Paraclete. Very recently, however, we have become much more aware of the Spirit's work in the world in and through other human beings. It is therefore time for each one of us to review the operations of this secret depth or leading edge of our personality, to understand how it has worked in our life, to come to terms with its weakness and its strength, and to learn from our own mistakes so that in the future, when we are "playing it by ear," we may be able to tell whether what we are hearing is a false spirit or the Paraclete who has come to teach us all truth.

21

And he said to them, "Go out to the whole world; proclaim the Good News to all creation. He who believes and is baptized will be saved; he who does not believe will be condemned. These are the signs that will be associated with believers: in my name they will cast out devils; they will have the gift of tongues; they will pick up snakes in their hands, and be unharmed should they drink deadly poison; they will lay their hands on the sick, who will recover."

And so the Lord Jesus, after he had spoken to them, was taken up into heaven: there at the right hand of God he took his place, while they, going out, preached everywhere, the Lord working with them and confirming the word by the signs that accompanied it.

Mark 16:15-20

DEPARTURE ceremonies for someone who has finished a job he has set out to do are curiously ambiguous and ambivalent affairs. General Washington bade farewell to his officers at the end of the Revolutionary War. His career, he thought, was finished; his service to his country was over. In departing for Mt. Vernon he left what he thought was a final testimony, his advice for the future of the Republic. A general leaves for a new command, a priest transfers to a new parish, an executive moves to a new job in a new city, a missionary returns home, a principal of a high school or a college president retires—all find themselves caught up in swirling and contradictory emotions.

They are sorry to leave, they are proud of their work and will miss their friends and followers, they are anxious about what will happen to those they leave behind; but they are looking forward to what lies ahead. They are both eager to leave and reluctant to go. And because life is made up of transitions, they do leave; there is no way a necessary transition can be postponed indefinitely. One must go about one's new task and leave others behind to continue the old.

The Ascension marks one of these ambiguous and ambivalent transitional experiences in the history of God's dealing with humans. The coming of Jesus, his life, his death, his resurrection, were the decisive events between the creation of the world and the final accomplishment of God's purpose. Indeed, Jesus represents the new creation; he is the new Adam, the father of a new humanity, the new Moses, leading humankind out of slavery into a life of freedom and hope, the new David, beginning God's new nation on earth. But like all events that occur in the course of human history, even this decisive intervention of God, perhaps the only really special movement of God into human affairs between the beginning and the end, between the alpha and the omega, had to come to a conclusion. Jesus himself would not stay among humans until the omega time; he would return to the Father in heaven. The work he began would continue, and he himself would continue at the work, but now through his friends and his followers, now through his people rather than directly by himself. The change was dramatic, decisive, and definitive. But for the apostles, it was a difficult and not altogether welcome challenge; and for Jesus, it was a time for a sad if temporary farewell.

The Ascension event, then, is not something distinct and separate from the Easter event. It is the conclusion of the visual impact of Easter; the Easter work has been done definitively once and for all, and now Jesus takes his temporary leave, says his temporary farewell. Easter will continue to have its impact but now invisibly through the work, the lives, the loves of the followers of Jesus. The feast of the Ascension symbolizes the fact that the time of Jesus is over; it is now the time of the church, it is now our time.

We may well wonder why. Would it not have been better —certainly it would have been far more efficient—for Jesus himself to stay around and continue to preach, continue to work his wonders, continue to exercise the magic of his personality, continue to draw people by the power of his union with the heavenly Father? And yet such a strategy simply is not the way God ordinarily works. He has his impact on the world through the normal course of events, nonhuman and human. He has set up the "game" in such a way as to maximize our freedom and the importance of our contribution. Were Jesus to have remained on earth the dignity and importance of our own mission would have been impaired.

In a certain sense, God broke his own rules by sending Jesus. (Some writers even refer to the Incarnation as "the sin" of God.) The rules were that he would work in the world through ordinary human events. But just to make sure that we get his point, he broke the rules once and sent someone who was by no means ordinary, his son Jesus. Once was enough; if we didn't get the point by way of the experience of Jesus, then we wouldn't get the point at all. One violation of the rules may have seemed justified to God, but he would not break them again. From now on the work was to be ours. The teaching of Jesus, the sacraments, the band of the followers of Jesus called the church would be there to continue the Easter event. Jesus himself would continue to work in the world but now through his followers. Any other strategy would not be fair to us, would not show the respect for our independence and integrity that God wants to show. If the feast of the Ascension is a feast of transition, a feast of change, a feast of the end of the time of Jesus and the beginning of the time of the church, it is also a feast which commemorates and celebrates God's vast respect for our dignity, our integrity, and the importance of our contribution.

Understandably, we feel ambivalent and uncertain about all this respect for our dignity and integrity. We wouldn't mind at all if God did a lot more of the work and relied much less on us. His rules are all well and good, but if he bent them once, why can't he keep on bending them? Why does he have to saddle us with the immense responsibility of continuing to reflect his love the way Jesus once did in the world? We would not be at all offended if he gave us a much less important role in his plans. But we argue with him in vain. As he said to our predecessor Job: "Were you around when I started this whole thing?" Like it or not, it's almost our game now as much as it is his.

22

"Father, the hour has come:
glorify your Son
so that your Son may glorify you;
and, through the power over all mankind that you
    have given him,
let him give eternal life to all those you have
    entrusted to him.
And eternal life is this:
to know you,
the only true God,
and Jesus Christ whom you have sent.
I have glorified you on earth
and finished the work
that you gave me to do.
Now, Father, it is time for you to glorify me
with that glory I had with you
before ever the world was.
I have made your name known
to the men you took from the world to give me.
They were yours and you gave them to me,
and they have kept your word.
Now at last they know
that all you have given me comes indeed from you;
for I have given them
the teaching you gave to me,
and they have truly accepted this, that I came from
    you,
and have believed that it was you who sent me.
I pray for them;
I am not praying for the world

but for those you have given me,
because they belong to you:
all I have is yours
and all you have is mine,
and in them I am glorified.
I am not in the world any longer,
but they are in the world,
and I am coming to you.
Holy Father,
keep those you have given me true to your name,
so that they may be one like us.

John 17:1-11

"PARTING," we are told, "is such sweet sorrow." When Shakespeare's audience first heard that line they must have thought it was remarkably insightful—if the crowd that went to his plays really took any of his poetry seriously. For they knew, of course, the sorrow of saying goodbye; they also knew that when the separation was not going to be permanent, the sorrow is mixed with a certain happiness that knows a reunion after a separation is one of the great joys of human experience. Separation and reunion deepen our friendship and love, so the sorrow of parting is made sweet in the anticipation of the "happy ending," the return, the reunion, and the deep affection which are at the end of the process of which parting is the beginning. In the complex "priestly prayer" of John's gospel Jesus guarantees a happy ending to his love affair with us.

Everybody seems to like happy endings except the movie critics. An unhappy ending, the critics seem to say, is realistic; that's the way life is; things go badly, and we might just as well face it, and not try to find escape from our implacable condition in entertainment. But those of us who pay the money to get into the theater or to buy the books like happy endings precisely because deep down in the human personality we have the absolutely unshakable conviction that the happy ending is not only more fun than the sorry ending but more true. If there were no happy endings to stories, it is very unlikely that we humans would bother about stories at all.

There is both tragedy and comedy in our human condition. Cheap, happy endings achieved without effort or travail are only mildly diverting. We expect our heroes and heroines to work and suffer for their eventual joy because we know that's the way it is. After we have had some experience of life we can absorb the truth that "they all lived happily ever after"—that marvelous line so loved by children—really means that they fought at least three times a week but no more than once a day. Our happiness in the human condition is never perfect; it is always spiced with sorrow and suffering, indeed is purchased through sorrow and suffering and made richer and more rewarding precisely because we have come through the agonies in order to arrive at the joy.

So we like our stories to be about joy after sorrow, happiness after pain, rebirth after death because we have the dogged conviction that that is what life is all about. A goodbye is sweet sorrow if we are confident that the goodbye is temporary, that the love which binds us together will be reborn stronger than ever after the period of separation is over. But then we are faced with the profound religious question, perhaps the only religious question that really matters, of whether our convictions about happy endings may not be the best single insight we have into what human life means and what human death is. Is our story, the story of each one of us, a romance which, after trial and suffering, ends happily, or is it an absurd tragedy in which our weakness, our frailty, our mistakes, our passions will bring us tumbling down to ultimate defeat? Will our lives end the way the critics think all stories should end? Is it possible that even the parting at death will turn out to be a sweet sorrow in retrospect, because it was nothing more than the beginning of a temporary interlude of separation after which love will be renewed, stronger and more vigorous than ever before?

John's gospel is the end of the story of Jesus—the temporary end from the point of view of us Christians but still the end. It is his "priestly prayer" recited in John's gospel at the Last Supper but appropriate at the end of Eastertime when we think of Jesus returned to the Father in heaven and sending the Holy Spirit to continue his work here on earth. We see Jesus taking his leave from his followers, pleading with the Father in heaven to lovingly guide and protect them until he returns. The "glory" of which he speaks does not mean a triumphant flash of light, it merely means his reputation. Jesus is praying that his reputation of having conquered death will remain with his followers and give them strength in the conviction that his story had a happy ending, and that the story of their lives will have happy endings too. There is the sweet sorrow of parting, too, in Jesus' final prayer for his followers, because he is convinced that they will meet again—"Down the road a bit," as Judge Roy Bean said in that very crazy movie. Death, we Catholic Christians firmly believe, is a separation which will end "down the road a bit."

It is a very great mistake to cover up, pretty up, to hide the awful, ugly evil of death. Christianity has suffered greatly from the attempts of some misguided enthusiasts to persuade ordinary human beings that death is just an illusion. We all live in great terror of death; it frightens us, it overwhelms us, it appalls us, it depresses us. It is certainly not an illusion; the crucifix is not an illusion. The Christian conviction is that death appears to be an illusion only in retrospect, and the retrospect has yet to come. Our conviction is not in a cheap, easy, happy ending, not in an Easter, an Ascension, or a Pentecost purchased without any Good Friday. Death may be *ultimately* an illusion, the ending may be *ultimately* happier, but there is much pain and suffering before the happiness. Therefore, we who are followers of Jesus who believe in the happy endings, must strive to balance the true symbols of cross and resurrection, of suffering and happiness, of parting and reunion. No one has to be persuaded that there is tragedy in life; it takes great faith to believe that beyond the tragedy there is reunion and happiness.

23

In the evening of that same day, the first day of the week, the doors were closed in the room where the disciples were, for fear of the Jews. Jesus came and stood among them. He said to them, "Peace be with you," and showed them his hands and his side. The disciples were filled with joy when they saw the Lord, and he said to them again, "Peace be with you. As the Father sent me, so am I sending you." After saying this he breathed on them and said:

> *"Receive the Holy Spirit.*
> *For those whose sins you forgive,*
> *they are forgiven;*
> *for those whose sins you retain,*
> *they are retained."*

John 20:19-23

A FLASH of lightning illuminates a dark street; you turn on a light at night, baffled as to just where you are, and see a familiar room; a single sentence, even a chance word, and another person reveals his or her whole personality; a gesture (like the pushing of a press secretary) or a facial expression and the nature of a politician is revealed; we ponder over a problem of mathematics or accounting or engineering or even over a jigsaw puzzle and all of a sudden we see how it fits; a great scientist watches mold grow in a culture and suddenly sees penicillin, the first wonder drug. These are quick, sharp, sudden illuminations, as transient as a blink of an eye; yet they reveal more about what is really going on than any amount of careful, reasoned, detailed explanation. In *logical learning* we work our way slowly, carefully, cautiously toward truth, but an insight we grasp all at once in a blinding flash.

Ordinarily life just slogs along. We are not mired in a swamp nor trapped in the Big Muddy all the time; we move along slowly, cautiously, carefully, leaning for support on the daily, monthly, yearly routine. The road is at least moderately smooth; if there is not much in the way of soul-challenging excitement, neither is there much in the way of tragic disappointment. The bumps, such as they are, are not too severe. There are no great highs, but then there are not all that many lows either. Life slips through our fingers that way, of course; we grow old before we know it. Youthful enthusiasm is gone, but then so is youthful disillusionment. We have put aside our capacity for wonder and surprise, but we have cut our losses in disappointment and betrayal. It may not be the best possible way to live, but it's a good way to survive, at least until the lights go out completely.

Occasionally, we are jarred out of our mediocrity, out of the routine of "this is the way we did it last year." It is like the flashing strobe light that seems to stop action in the brilliant glare of its intermittent illumination. Something happens: We are caught by a phrase in a book, a few words from scripture suddenly stick in our mind, an old friend reappears, an opportunity is offered us, an invitation is issued, a smile is flashed, a whole new idea crosses our minds. We see briefly, momentarily, as in a flash of lightning, an array of exciting, worrying, scary, but exhilarating possibilities. Things do not have to be the way they are; they can be different—better, more thrilling, more fascinating, more frightening, perhaps, but also more fun. The question becomes not who turned the lights off but who turned them on. For in those brief flashes of illumination, which occur in the life of everyone, we realize that most of the time we are groping in the dark, coming from where we know not and going to where we have not the slightest idea.

On Pentecost Sunday, at least, it is clear who threw the switch: it is the poltergeist God, the playful Spirit, the God of pranks and practical jokes, the God of variety, diversity, heterogeneity. It is not the God who creates but the God who calls, the God who flirts with us, the God who leads us on, the God who tries to attract us, the God who is not above seducing us if we give him half a chance. The warm, appealing, friendly God, beckoning us down the road, calling us from across the river, pleading with us to wade out and join him on the other side. It is this Spirit who speaks to our spirit, the fine, leading edge of God talking to the fine, leading edge of our own personality, pleading with us to be true to all that is unique, special, creative, spontaneous, and outgoing in ourselves. It is a dancing God, who invites us to dance with him, who tries to trick us into running down the road with him.

One way of thinking about the Blessed Trinity is that it is the Father who creates things and sets them in motion, it is the Son who is the Hound of Heaven that pursues us down the highway, and it is the Holy Spirit who lays in wait either to trip us up so that the Son can catch up to us or to urge us to run faster so that with our energies and resources pushed to the breaking point we finally become not just someone like everyone else but someone very special—ourselves. Does all this seem wild and impossible? How can the Holy Spirit be a prankster, a trickster, a poltergeist? How can he possibly be lying in wait for us to trick us? How can he be trying to seduce us to join him on the other side of the magic wall? Isn't that most ungodlike behavior? And what did Nietzsche mean when he said that the only God worth believing in is a dancing God?

But if we don't think the Holy Spirit is a trickster, a God who calls forth that which is most special and unique in each of us, then how do we explain Pentecost? The apostles were tricked, led on, seduced; they were the victims of one of history's great practical jokes. There they were in the upper room, praying on the morning of the first day of the week, minding their own business, not troubling anybody; indeed they were being very careful not to trouble anybody. So what happened? The Holy Spirit sneaked into the upper room and turned them on almost as though he had put acid in their food. The Holy Spirit played his splendid practical joke, and the church came into the world; and the apostles, once they had let their true selves out into the open, knew that there would be no turning back ever again. The God who calls had called them so vigorously, so insistently, that without knowing it they had responded.

It's a terrible thing, the scripture says, to fall into the hands of the living God. By that the bible means that once you have fallen into God's hands, once he has tricked you, once he has seduced you into being your real self, there's no turning back because you don't want to turn back; it's too much fun being the one you really are. So, on Pentecost, as all of us do our best to avoid the dancing God who wants to trick us into a dance, it is appropriate to ask ourselves, who would we be and what would we do if we were who we really are?

24

Yes, God loved the world so much
that he gave his only Son,
so that everyone who believes in him may not be lost
but may have eternal life.
For God sent his Son into the world
not to condemn the world,
but so that through him the world might be saved.
No one who believes in him will be condemned;
but whoever refuses to believe is condemned already,
because he has refused to believe
in the name of God's only Son.

John 3:16-18

IT is the end of a frustrating and foolish day. We are tired, weary, exhausted. We woke up with a headache, rush-hour traffic was bad, dinner was burned, we were dragged away from our favorite television program by one of those intolerable phone calls which we know, by the sound of the voice, will take at least a half-hour. It's been a long, hard winter and spring was no prize either. The savor has gone out of life; nothing seems exciting, nothing worth caring about. We wander from day to day in a frustrating routine, responding to pressures and balancing conflicting responsibilities. Is this the life that beckoned with such promise when we were young and enthusiastic? What went wrong?

It is not malicious sin or monstrous immorality that destroys most of us. It is the monotonous routine of every day. We do not do much that is wrong, mostly, it seems, because we don't do much at all. We try, we struggle, we tread water yet we barely stay afloat. The great shocking sin doesn't seem even to be an option for us anymore. Life is a drag, as the teen-agers say, a drag in the literal sense of the word. It pulls us down, wears us out, beats us into the ground. It is an enervating treadmill to oblivion. We wear ourselves out doing nothing. We waste our time on silly rivalries, crazy feuds and senseless projects which, even if they succeed, will make little difference to anybody. It is not so much that we want to quit—even that seems to be beyond our capabilities. The only goal left is to deaden the pain.

Then along comes Trinity Sunday. The feast is explicitly and deliberately designed to dazzle, delight, and challenge us. It is a feast filled with splendor and mysticism, glory and transcendence, a feast which is supposed to snap us out of our routine, shake us up, and give us a new perspective, invigorate, renew and restore us. What happens? For all too many of us, nothing. We hear many strange mystifying words in a language which we suppose is English but which does not communicate anything to us. Trinity Sunday is a Sunday just like any other Sunday; it has no particular impact on our lives.

The catechetics of the past have destroyed for many people the greatness of the feast. The Trinity was something we had to believe under pain of mortal sin. It was a contradiction in terms, a logical puzzle which we could almost figure out but not quite. It was a test of our faith. There are enough tests in life, enough bafflements, enough incomprehensible events; we don't need another one. We accept the doctrine of the Trinity because it is part of our faith, but deep down inside we often find ourselves wondering, who needs a triune God?

In fact, the doctrine of the Trinity is not a puzzle, not

a test, not a challenge to faith; it is a dazzling revelation, an insight into the way things really are, a hint of a mystical experience, a breaking through to that which is beneath, beyond and above all. It is a dizzying, dazzling, overwhelming phenomenon. Yahweh comes down from the mountain and stands with Moses; Jesus tells us that we will not die; Paul proclaims that God's love and Jesus' grace and the community of the Holy Spirit are all around us. Even though our lives may seem deadly dull, even though there does not seem much worth living for, the doctrine of the Trinity proclaims bravely and vigorously that there are mighty and wondrous events going on. Trinity Sunday is intended to reawaken our sense of wonder and awe, to resensitize us, and to assert the excitement of human life and love.

God was not content to merely create this technicolor world of ours to reveal his own goodness and graciousness; he was afraid that we might miss the point. So, to make sure we wouldn't, he sent his son Jesus to make things doubly clear to us, to reveal that the one really bad thing in the world, death, would not have the final word. Jesus in his turn promised that the Holy Spirit would come to continue his work. God, if he has any faults at all, errs by excess. He created once, then to make his point again, he sent Jesus to begin a recreated humanity, and then just in case we missed the message, the Holy Spirit came to recreate each one of us every day of our lives.

In the language of the time of Jesus, the great mystery of God's love was often presented in the image of the sinful human and forgiving God. The prodigal son story is the most beautiful example of this imagery. But the same idea might better be conveyed in our time by the image of the creative person and the calling God. Each of us has been blessed by God with abilities and capacities to give, to love, to trust, to live. The Lord God calls us to give ourselves to him and to become the best we are capable of being in order that we might love effectively. We have all too frequently refused to respond to his invitation, and that is sin; but he forgives our sin and continues to call us. On this feast of the most holy Trinity, let us ask ourselves, very pointedly, whether we are truly living up to the potential that God has given us. Do those who are closest to us think that each day we are growing in our goodness and generosity?

25

On the first day of Unleavened Bread, when the Passover lamb was sacrificed, his disciples said to him, Where do you want us to go and make the preparations for you to eat the passover? So he sent two of his disciples, saying to them, "Go into the city and you will meet a man carrying a pitcher of water. Follow him, and say to the owner of the house which he enters, "The Master says: Where is my dining room in which I can eat the passover with my disciples? He will show you a large upper room furnished with couches, all prepared. Make the preparations for us there." The disciples set out and went to the city and found everything as he had told them, and prepared the Passover.

Mark 14:12-16

LET'S have a fight. Things have been quiet, dull and peaceful for too long. What good is a close personal relationship without a fight? Fighting is fun; it lets off steam, releases aggression, makes everybody feel good and when the fight ends, there's the extra fun of reconciliation—if reconciliation works. So, all right, let's have a fight. What's the best time to have it? Well, the supper hour, of course. What better time for everybody in the family to blow their tops at everyone else. Everyone is tense, nervous, exhausted after the day; everyone feels put upon, neglected, unappreciated, pushed around; in short, everyone is spoiling for a fight. Of course, the supper hour is the time when we are supposed to join together in love. Fine. Let the rest of those so-and-sos love *me* for a change. Right now, I'll make them prove they care about me by starting a rip-roaring, wing-ding of a fight.

Nobody really thinks like that, you say? Well, maybe they don't, but they certainly act as though they do often enough. It seems that everybody saves up their frustrations, aggressions, angers, discontents, dissatisfactions and just plain orneriness to spill out on the supper table. And it goes beyond families; lovers and friends often stage their most spectacular arguments while sitting around a table. The act of coming together and sharing a meal—the most primitive and primordial ratification and celebration of human community—is effectively turned into a denial and perhaps a destruction of community. Maybe people don't do it deliberately, maybe they are not all that perverse; but they do it, and they do it so often and so predictably and systematically that you almost have to believe, deep down inside, most of them (or most of us) know exactly what they're doing. If you really want to "get" to the other person, the meal table is the place to do it.

During Passover dinner it was revealed that one of Jesus' friends was systematically scheming to betray him. The rest of his friends were, in their hearts, wondering about available escape hatches for themselves should things go wrong before the sun rose the next morning. Jesus surely knew the risks he was taking by staying in Jerusalem after dark. It was a dangerous thing to do, and even if he weren't prudent, you can bet your last dollar most of the other members of his band were; and while they told him and one another (even themselves, probably) that they wouldn't dream of running, just the same, there isn't much doubt (especially in light of their subsequent behavior) that they had escape plans very clearly worked out. The

Last Supper was like many other family meals—a strange, ambivalent event which celebrated unity and love but was blighted by suspicion and distrust.

In the gospel passage we hear Mark effectively connect the Last Supper with the cross, for the cross—the betrayal of love—was already present at the Last Supper. Indeed, the cross is present at almost every communal eating situation, because while it is love that brings people together to share a common meal, hatred accompanies love; and there is always the possibility that hatred will rear its head and strike during the meal—if not to vanquish love at least to weaken it. The real cross of human love is that we must respect in our love the freedom of others, and as long as others are free, they will hurt us—perhaps unintentionally and clumsily, or perhaps deliberately and viciously. It does not mean that they do not love us; it simply means that they are confused, angry, frightened and inept. For all their pathetic eagerness to love, they really don't know how to go about it. The biggest cross in love is the people we love, and the biggest cross for the people who love us is ourselves.

But we do not turn away from those we love because they have the power to hurt us and on occasion in fact do hurt us. For love means giving despite the hurt that is received, and it means knowing that we will be accepted despite the hurt that we give. The line in the movie was wrong: Love *does* mean we have to say we're sorry. Indeed, we have to say it every day of a loving life together. What love means is that when we say we're sorry, we know we will be forgiven; and when we hear another say he or she is sorry to us, we will forgive. Part of the cross of our love is not only suffering for others but having to forgive them. The first Eucharistic meal at the Passover banquet was a love feast in the fullest sense of the word. It had joy, hope, affection and commitment, but it also had pain, sorrow, hurt and forgiveness.

So our Eucharist, our Last Supper, our community banquet, the Mass has a continuity with all our family meals. There is misunderstanding, tension, conflict beneath the surface, together with the love and the friendship and the commitment. At Mass we celebrate our human predicament: We want to love; we end up hurting. We want to be friends; we end up fighting. We want to share resurrection and we stir up guilt, generate conflict and behave meanly to those we love. And we suffer from their meanness in return. We come to Mass not as innocents but as sinners; we come to Mass as those who have been responsible for the cross. But we also come to Mass as those who have forgiven, who have been forgiven. We come to Mass as those who know that the love and affection we celebrate at Mass is stronger than the hatred and the pain which is inevitably present. Good Friday and Easter Sunday are present every time we gather around the Eucharistic banquet table, and we go forth from Mass at the end strengthened, reinforced, reinvigorated, full of hope and confidence and joy, because we know that resurrection is stronger than the cross. And the love that Jesus felt for his disciples at the Last Supper, the love we feel for those with whom we share a common meal, is stronger than the hatred which causes the cross.

The Mass is a sacrament, a revelation of God's love and forgiveness, of resurrection triumphing over suffering. It can only have meaning for us if we are ready to forgive. Should we come to church with unforgiveness in our hearts, then the Mass is a mockery, a caricature. On the Feast of Corpus Christi, when we celebrate a unity that is fractured and restored, a friendship that has been broken and reconciled, we must examine our hearts and see what unforgiveness is still present, and before the sun goes down once again, we should begin to replace unforgiveness with forgiveness, hatred with love.

26

And when he saw the crowds he felt sorry for them because they were harassed and dejected, like sheep without a shepherd. Then he said to his disciples, "The harvest is rich but the laborers are few, so ask the Lord of the harvest to send laborers to his harvest."

He summoned his twelve disciples, and gave them authority over unclean spirits with power to cast them out and to cure all kinds of diseases and sickness.

These are the names of the twelve apostles: first, Simon who is called Peter, and his brother Andrew; James the son of Zebedee, and his brother John; Philip and Bartholomew; Thomas, and Matthew the tax collector; James the son of Alphaeus, and Thaddaeus; Simon the Zealot and Judas Iscariot, the one who was to betray him. These twelve Jesus sent out, instructing them as follows:

"Do not turn your steps to pagan territory, and do not enter any Samaritan town; go rather to the lost sheep of the House of Israel. And as you go, proclaim that the kingdom of heaven is close at hand. Cure the sick, raise the dead, cleanse the lepers, cast out devils. You received without charge, give without charge."

Matthew 9:36-10:8

THE poet Hilaire Belloc was not altogether immune from a nasty strain of anti-Semitism. One of his "cautionary verses" read: "How odd/ Of God/ To Choose/ The Jews." There was, perhaps, a grudging confession in that verse that Belloc's anti-Semitism was wrong, because even if he didn't like the Jews, God did. A more appropriate line, though it doesn't rhyme so cleverly, would be: "How odd/ Of God/ To choose/ Any of us/ Much less/ All of us." For we are not particularly attractive creatures—rigid, suspicious, contentious, haughty, stubborn, mean, arrogant, nasty, cynical, dyspeptic. What does God see in us anyway?

Yet God has fallen in love with us—the long, the short and the tall, the good, bad, and most of the rest of us who are only indifferent. Christ died for us even though we were still sinners. It is precisely by this that God proves his love for us. Jesus was moved with pity, according to the gospel, because he saw the crowds lying prostrate from exhaustion like sheep without a shepherd. In order that he might more effectively exercise his affection for us, Jesus appointed the apostles to help him in his work, and Scripture makes it clear that God chose us; he fell in love with us long before the thought even occurred to us of loving him in return.

God chose us, all of us, with the same sort of wild, spontaneous freedom with which Jesus chose his first twelve followers. He saw us with all our faults, all our weaknesses, and our phoniness, all our inconsistencies and loved us anyhow. Love is not blind, despite the proverb; love sees more clearly than anything else. It is well aware of faults but doesn't care enough to stop loving.

Whether our apostolate is the general apostolate of all Christians or the special assignment of priests and religious, the most difficult enemy we face is discouragement. Instead of being shepherd to the leaderless sheep, it is easy for us to become just one member of the disorganized flock. We lose confidence in ourselves, in our mission, in the message of Jesus, in God. It is precisely at this time, of course, that we need to renew and refresh our faith in the Chief Shepherd and in the Lord of the Harvest. Anyone who thinks he or she can work as an apostle without frequently returning to God and asking for deeper, richer and stronger faith is merely deceiving himself or herself.

There is considerable risk that when we speak of God's loving us the way a boy and girl care for one another when they fall in love, the way a man and woman who have shared life together for many years love each other, that we will be engaging in some wild poetic exaggeration. God's love obviously can't be like the hungering intensity of two mature lovers who have shared life for many years, nor can it be like the spontaneous recklessness of two young lovers who have discovered love for the first time. It's a nice image to say that God has fallen in love with us, but God clearly can't and doesn't do that sort of thing.

In fact, however, the image of God falling in love with us fails not because it is too exaggerated but because it is too cautious—it does not overstate the case but rather it understates it. The whole burden of the scriptures, Old and New Testaments alike, and the Christian tradition ever since the coming of Jesus has been that God's love for us is more passionate, more reckless, more hungry, more intense, more uninhibited than human passion. When we say that God has fallen in love with us, we mean that he acts toward us like human lovers do toward one another, *only more so.*

To the Israelites, whom Moses led out of Egypt, this passionately loving God was something of an embarrassment. Unlike the gods of their neighbors, who stayed aloof, independent, and uninvolved on their mountaintops, Yahweh came part way down the mountain to deal with his people. He, not they, took the initiative; he intervened in their lives rather than wait for them to intervene in his solitude. He announced, unasked and uninvited and fre-

117

quently unwanted, "I am Yahweh, your God." In that single sentence he proclaimed his intervention in the human condition and pledged his love to us. It was very odd of him indeed, but the whole revelation is summarized in that single pledge of love. All else, when it comes down to it, is commentary and explanation.

There is no more exciting experience in life than to discover that someone else loves you. Our faces grow warm, heads drop, the blood courses rapidly through our veins, our hearts feel like they will break out of our rib cages. We are loved and our personalities fill with joy. We may not be able to have (except occasionally) the same set of experiences when we understand that God loves us, that God indeed has fallen in love with each one of us. Still, that is our faith, that is why Jesus came to the world. It was to reveal this, Paul tells us, that he died on the cross. Today we can at least ask ourselves how our lives would change if we really believed that our very odd God was in love with us.

27

When Jesus had crossed again in the boat to the other side, a large crowd gathered round him and he stayed by the lakeside. Then one of the synagogue officials came up, Jairus by name, and seeing him, fell at his feet and pleaded with him earnestly, saying, "My little daughter is desperately sick. Do come and lay your hands on her to make her better and save her life." Jesus went with him and a large crowd followed him; they were pressing all round him.

Now there was a woman who had suffered from a hemorrhage for twelve years; after long and painful treatment under various doctors, she had spent all she had without being any the better for it, in fact, she was getting worse. She had heard about Jesus, and she came up behind him through the crowd and touched his cloak. "If I can touch even his clothes," she had told herself, "I shall be well again." And the source of the bleeding dried up instantly, and she felt in herself that she was cured of her complaint. Immediately aware that power had gone out from him, Jesus turned round in the crowd and said, "Who touched my clothes?" His disciples said to him, "You see how the crowd is pressing round you and yet you say, 'Who touched me?'" But he continued to look all round to see who had done it. Then the woman came forward, frightened and trembling because she knew what had happened to her, and she fell at his feet and told him the whole truth. "My daughter," he said, "your faith has restored you to health; go in peace and be free from your complaint."

While he was still speaking some people arrived from the house of the synagogue official to say, "Your daughter *is dead: why put the Master to any further trouble?" But Jesus had overheard this remark of theirs and he said to the official, "Do not be afraid; only have faith." And he allowed no one to go with him except Peter and James and John the brother of James. So they came to the official's house and Jesus noticed all the commotion, with people weeping and wailing unrestrainedly. He went in and said to them, "Why all this commotion and crying? The child is not dead, but asleep." But they laughed at him. So he turned them all out and, taking with him the child's father and mother and his own companions, he went into the place where the child lay. And taking the child by the hand he said to her, "Talitha, kum!" which means, "Little girl, I tell you to get up." The little girl got up at once and began to walk about, for she was twelve years old. At this they were overcome with astonishment, and he ordered them strictly not to let anyone know about it, and told them to give her something to eat.*

Mark 5:21-43

A NUMBER of books have appeared in the last thirty years that say it is impossible to believe in God's goodness after the concentration camps and Hiroshima. If six million people can die in places like Dachau and Buchanwald, if one hundred thousand can die in one exploding bomb, how can one possibly believe in a loving God? One need not minimize the evil ugliness of concentration camps and saturation bombing to observe that the real problem is not the death of six million people but the death of one child. If God permits even one innocent child to die, how can he be good? One or six million isn't all that much different as far as the problem goes. If the daughter of Jairus could die how can there be any good in the universe?

One of the most heart-rending places in the world is a children's hospital, particularly those wards which hold very sick and fatally ill children. To the last, each is graced with the playfulness, the vitality, the spark of life that makes them so attractive. And when we see this life linked with the cold, bleak prospect of death we wince with pain. It isn't fair. This life should not be snuffed out in child-hood. Why do we think that? Why does death seem so unfair when a child is afflicted with it? Perhaps the answer is that death at the end of a long or even moderate life span seems less unjust. One has experienced the joys and satisfactions of being an adult; but the dying child will never experience them. Besides, we adults have done things wrong, we have lost our innocence; we "deserve" to die; the little child has done nothing wrong. Why should children have to die?

But in fact, this reasoning is deceptive. No one deserves to die; no matter how many mistakes and evil deeds we are responsible for, the snuffing out of our existence by the destructive annihilation of death is disproportionate to what we have done wrong. And no matter how long our lives have been, they have not been long enough; there are still other things to do, other joys and happinesses to be experienced. Death is just ugly, evil, absurd and vicious.

Through the course of human history, most people have died young. The life expectancy rate for a child at birth, even in relatively recent times, was only twenty-five years. One quarter of all children born died in the first year of life. Even in the last century, tens of thousands of children were the victims of infanticide, killed by their own parents who simply could not feed another mouth. Such a slaughter of innocents has been part of the human condition, apparently, from the very beginning. Gerbils eat their surplus children; human beings are not quite that savage, but when war or plague do not destroy excess children, the ordinary human custom has been for the parents to do it one way or another. This fact is as terrifying as it is true and one might well ask how could a good God permit such slaughter, such an ongoing massacre perpetrated by humankind that makes Dachau and Hiroshima seem minor by comparison. If the death of one child is inexplicable and the sight of a dying child intolerable, what can one say to the systematic and customary murder of infants? Can there be any good in a world where such things happen?

And so the daughter of Jairus was brought back from the dead—or cured from a fatal illness, as some scripture writers now argue. What can saving the life of one such little girl mean in the face of the loss of so many little girls? And so the daughter of Jairus lived a little longer. How much longer? To her twenty-fifth birthday—a normal life span then? Or did she live to the age we would consider middle? Perhaps, like a few in her time, she lived to what we would call old age. Did she marry the son of the widow of Naim, as pious Christian sentiment once maintained? Did she have children and grandchildren of her own? Whatever may have happened to little Ms. Jairus, she died again—and this time definitively. There was no Jesus around to bring her back to life. So what was the point of it all? It was good of Jesus to give her those extra years, one supposes. But how good? How important were they? After all, they merely prolonged one life and only postponed the advent of death. Ms. Jairus lived on borrowed time for a few more years than she otherwise would have. Is there anything in this worth being terribly impressed about?

The answer is that the few extra years of life for the daughter of Jairus, as important as they surely were to her, her family and her friends, find their way into scripture not to represent a single gracious marvel but to be a sign of a deeper and richer marvel. If we were to ask Jesus what was the point of prolonging the life of Jairus' daughter for a few years, his response would doubtless be that what happened there in her house was but a hint of what was to come. Just as he brought the little girl back to life on the spot, he would at some later date bring her and all the other little children and all the other adults and everyone who had ever suffered and died upon the planet earth back to life. The raising of Jairus's daughter was a signal of victory, evidence that sin and death would not utter the last word about human life and human love, that no power on earth was strong enough to snuff out the human spirit once it has been joined to the Heavenly Father in love. Why postpone the death of a little girl? Because death itself was being conquered.

The Easter season is over, and we settle down for the ordinary Sundays of the year. And how does the church begin? By returning boldly and dramatically to the Easter theme: Life conquers death. Once again we are asked to commit ourselves to that core message of Christianity, to believe that what happened to the little girl when Jesus walked into her house will eventually happen to us. We should also ask ourselves, do we really live in such a way that those who know us could tell immediately that we believe Jesus has won a victory for us over death.

28

At that time Jesus exclaimed, "I bless you, Father, Lord of heaven and earth, for hiding these things from the learned and the clever and revealing them to mere children. Yes, Father, for that is what it pleased you to do. Everything has been entrusted to me by my Father; and no one knows the Son except the Father, just as no one knows the Father except the Son and those to whom the Son chooses to reveal him.

"Come to me, all you who labor and are overburdened, and I will give you rest. Shoulder my yoke and learn from me, for I am gentle and humble in heart, and you will find rest for your souls. *Yes, my yoke is easy and my burden light."*

Matthew 11:25-30

THE founder of modern India was a man named Gandhi (no relation, incidentally, to the former prime minister, Indira Gandhi). He was one of the most extraordinary men of the twentieth century, an eminent lawyer who returned to India after living in South Africa, a man who practiced voluntary celibacy even though he was married, a strict vegetarian, a holy man, and a master practitioner of non-violent politics. Gandhi forced the English out of India without ever causing a drop of English blood to be shed. Whatever killing took place was done by others to his followers; Gandhi himself ultimately died a martyr, assassinated by a religious extremist—a strangely ironic end for a man who absolutely eschewed all violence. His last act before he died was to extend a gesture of forgiveness to his assassin.

Gandhi made mistakes, as do all humans; yet he displayed, as few have in the twentieth century, the ability of meekness to become extraordinary strength. Many people compare the late Dr. Martin Luther King to Gandhi, and while all comparisons of this nature are bound to have their defects, it is certainly true that King preached nonviolence and did his best to practice it. Ironically, he, too, died a violent death; his death was abhorrent to everything he preached. In retrospect, however, King, a nonviolent man, accomplished more than all the violent, hate-filled men and women (white and black) who came after him.

Weakness, then, is strength, weakness is power, gentleness is might, tenderness is devastating. That is the message not only of Matthew's gospel, where it is explicit, but of the whole gospel, the whole life and ministry and teaching of Jesus. You may be able to compel people to do your will by force, but you will only win them to your cause by meekness and gentleness. Some people are offended when Jesus is compared to Gandhi, and even more when he is compared to Dr. King; but such a comparison has nothing to do with the particular political policies, wisdom, or lack of wisdom of the two men. Both of them, according to their lights, tried to live what they thought was the message of Jesus (Gandhi drawing a parallel message from his own religious tradition, but being very well aware that it was parallel to the message of Jesus). One makes the comparison not to canonize either Gandhi or Dr. King but rather to point out the enormous strength that is to be found in meekness and the tremendous impact on other human beings of the person who is meek and humble of heart, who is self-disciplined, gentle, and absolutely refuses to be taken over by violence, hatred, vindictiveness, anger, vengefulness. The person who wants revenge is weak, the vindictive person is powerless, the angry man or woman has no strength, the domineering person is pathetically unable to cope.

In our lives we have all encountered such men and women of self-esteem, self-discipline, self-control. They are truly meek, not passive-aggressive doormats who invite us to stamp on them and then manipulate our guilt, but calm, strong, vigorous men and women whose meekness is the result of courage, resourcefulness, discipline, and energy, as well as enormous personal power. Jesus said elsewhere that the meek inherit the earth. As someone said ironically, "If the meek don't inherit the earth, then no one else will, because there won't be an earth to inherit."

Such a statement is probably an exaggeration. It is wrong to equate meekness with passivity or powerlessness. The meek person has power over others because first of all meek persons have power over themselves. When meek men or women turn their cheek it is not because they are afraid to fight back, it is because they know that turning the other cheek is an effective way of disarming the enemy and inviting him to become a friend.

The late Saul Alinsky once said to Dorothy Day, "Non-violence is an effective strategy." It is more than that, of course, though it is surely that, precisely because it is the strongest human way to react. Jesus was meek and humble of human heart; he was the strongest of humans, and therefore the most effective of humans strategically. He won, not by brute strength, not by the raw power of his voice, not by his ability to manipulate, dominate, control, and over-awe but by being meek, gentle, and humble of heart, by imposing on his friends the yoke that was easy, a burden that was light because it was a yoke shared with one who loved them. The meek will inherit the earth because they are the most effective strategists and because they are the strongest of humans.

The burden of Jesus is light and the yoke is easy because the peace he seeks is a peace that comes from being able to accept God's love and open ourselves up to serving others with generosity and concern. The Messiah, however, does not bring us peace by eliminating self-discipline or by eradicating all problems from our lives. The very efforts we expend on focusing our energies and our talents and on overcoming problems and trials become a source of joy and peace to us because we engage in such efforts in the name of Jesus and with his help. Yet, we must remember that carrying the burden which Jesus imposes on us and accepting his yoke does not *earn* for us the love of Jesus and the heavenly Father. Our efforts are required not to win God's love but rather to witness that love to others and persuade them to accept that same love.

If we are not meek, if we are hot-tempered, quick-tongued, vindictive, angry, the reason is that we are weak, powerless, insecure, threatened, afraid. Let us ask ourselves today, what is that abiding theme of weakness, that strain of insecurity that runs through our own personalities that forces us to try to dominate other human beings by raw power instead of winning them by being gentle and humble of heart?

29

He made a tour round the villages, teaching. Then he summoned the Twelve and began to send them out in pairs giving them authority over the unclean spirits. And he instructed them to take nothing for the journey except a staff—no bread, no haversack, no coppers for their purses. They were to wear sandals but, he added, "Do not take a spare tunic." And he said to them, "If you enter a house anywhere, stay there until you leave the district. And if any place does not welcome you and people refuse to listen to you, as you walk away shake off the dust from under your feet as a sign to them." So they set off to preach repentance; and they cast out many devils, and anointed many sick people with oil and cured them.

Mark 6:7-13

THE older we get the harder it is to move. It is not merely that we are more strongly wedded to our habits and our routines, though that is surely part of it; but moving itself gets harder each time because there are simply more things to move. As we journey through life we pile up more and more material goods, and each time we change our residence we have to pack and unpack them. Sometimes we even wonder what is going to happen to all our boxes of things after we have left the world. We don't use much of the stuff we have; how can we expect anyone else to? In Mark's gospel the Lord told his apostles to travel light. It's an attractive idea, but most of us travel very heavy indeed.

We all secretly admire the young person or the seasoned traveler who is able to sling a flight bag over his or her shoulder or pack a very small carry-on briefcase and depart on a trip, carefree and relaxed. No heavy bags to be carried, no porters to be tipped, no endless hassling by customs and security inspectors. That was, we realize, the way our ancestors traveled when they moved from one hunting ground to another. Not having many things, they had no choice but to travel lightly. We have a lot of things, and traveling lightly is a choice but not one we make very often. Yet, the mountain of boxes which the moving van must pick up or the vast amount of luggage which accompanies us on our vacations are really not the problem. Traveling lightly in the sense of Mark's gospel is not a matter of physical baggage; the real question is not how much we have but how much we are tied down.

How can we tell whether we have accumulated unnecessary baggage on our journey through life? Probably the best, quickest and easiest reality test is to ask how many things we own which we never use, have not used for a long time, and probably will never use again. If the number is high, we have accumulated excess baggage, and we must ask ourselves, do we save these things to use or merely to have them? If the latter is the case, then maybe we have troubles.

Why was the Lord Jesus so concerned about his apostles not being encumbered by heavy baggage? The answer is that he wanted them to move quickly and decisively because they were on an urgent mission. Time was short; there was a message to be preached. It had to be done quickly before time ran out. The message was that God's love was being manifested in a special and dramatic way, that he was "breaking into" the ordinary course of human events in the life and preaching of Jesus. Caught up in this "eschatological urgency," there simply wasn't any time to waste packing and unpacking and lugging heavy burdens along with them. Time was running out; there was a need to hurry.

Although the instruction was fitted to the particular time and place, the underlying theme is as relevant to us as it was to the followers of Jesus. We have, relatively speaking, only a little time on earth, a little time to fulfill our mission, to live our lives in such a way that others may learn from us the joy and confidence and trust that comes from believing in God's all powerful love and implacable fidelity to us. There is nothing wrong with material possessions; one can have televisions and stereos and sailboats and cars and all those other splendid good things that God has enabled human ingenuity to create. Catholic Christianity is not puritanical or Manichaean; we do not believe material things are wrong. On the contrary, if the use of them enables us to have a fuller, deeper, and more authentic human life, they are not only good in themselves but good for us. They become a problem only when they dominate us.

Nevertheless, while Christianity rejects the notion that worldly goods are in themselves evil, it still is very careful to make clear that like most other good things, it is very easy for humans to misunderstand and misuse them. We can easily become trapped in our material possessions, burdened down by them, overwhelmed by them. We are not their master; we become their slave. We love our dignity, our freedom. We are not fast on our feet, mobile; we can't play it by ear because all the things we have around us slow us down, impede us, and their noise drowns out the whisperings of the Holy Spirit who guides us when we play it by ear. The ultimate trick that material goods play on us is to make us think that the possession of them can provide security and happiness. There is nothing in the things to create this deception; it is rather a flaw in us.

The old line preaches that you can't take it with you—no matter what "it" is; deep down we know that's true. But sometimes we think we would rather like to try. One can travel lightly through life only if one is really and truly confident of God's loving and tender care. If we don't believe that, then we will pile up material things, aware perhaps that we can't bring them along with us, but still gathering them around us, huddling among them, trying pathetically to hide from our ultimate destiny. And the material things may not protect us from death, but they may at least postpone it, or hide its face from us, or so beguile us with their pleasures and delight that for a while we do not think of death. It is a terrible, gruesome, pathetic way to live. The choice is very simple: Either we love and trust God, place our security in him and travel lightly, using material goods as we need and enjoy them; or we lack such trust and hide behind our accumulated possessions, trying vainly to escape our mortality.

How many things do we have that we never use? Why do we have so many? What secrets about our own acquisitive personality, our own lack of confidence, our own existential insecurity do our vast amounts of possessions reveal to us? How much of our time and effort, energy and concern is focused on the things that are ours? Do these things interfere with our loving service of others and our commitment to God?

30

In the course of their journey he came to a village, and a woman named Martha welcomed him into her house. She had a sister called Mary, who sat down at the Lord's feet and listened to him speaking. Now Martha who was distracted with all the serving said, "Lord, do you not care that my sister is leaving me to do the serving all by myself? Please tell her to help me." But the Lord answered: "Martha, Martha," he said, "you worry and fret about so many things, and yet few are needed, indeed only one. It is Mary who has chosen the better part; it is not to be taken from her."

Luke 10:38-42

WE rush through life. We hurry so we won't be late for school; we push to beat the rush hour going to and from work; we are late for appointments because we have so many things to do; we rush to catch the train; we are late for weddings, baptisms, dinners, parties, graduations; and if there were a way to arrange it, we would be late for our own funeral. Why are we late? Because we are in such a hurry. And why are we in such a hurry? Because we have so many things to do. Life is a mixture of hurrying, rushing, being late, and arriving wherever we are going, tardy and breathless. Why?

Back in the old days there used to be arguments in Catholic circles about whether the active life was superior to the contemplative life. Those who belonged in the contemplative religious order used to insist that their life was superior to that of those in the active orders, because they were following the path of Mary, and the others were following the path of Martha. Then Thomas Aquinas came along and suggested that superior to both the active and the contemplative were those communities that combined both. It just happened that his own Dominican order was a combination of the two. Nowadays such arguments are deemed frivolous, especially since the question now is not active versus contemplative but rather whether the religious life can survive. However; old Thomas Aquinas was still right. Jesus was not trying to tell us that those who followed the way of Mary were superior to those who followed the way of Martha. Rather, he was trying to tell us that there ought to be some of Martha and some of Mary in any fully developed and authentic life.

Whatever is to be said about other periods of human history, at the present time the Martha in each one of us is hardly repressed. There are a few people in the United States today who are too contemplative, too reflective, too meditative, too spiritual. Parish priests do not have to preach on Sunday urging-people to greater activity; they do not have to warn their parishioners that it is unwise to spend all day, every day rapt in contemplation or pursuing mystical disciplines. There may be some young people who have given up on the world and have retreated into communes as a way of "dropping out," but most of us don't drop out, and even those who do don't stay out for very long. Before much time has passed, the typical dropout is likely to be back, bustling through life with the Martha aspect of his or her personality in full control.

No, the real problem is just the other way. Our lives are so insanely active that few of us are willing to permit ourselves enough time to play the Mary role. Thinking, contemplating, reflecting, meditating are all attractive and pleasant activities; but we simply don't have the time to "waste" on such things. We have to hurry, because if we don't, we'll be late. There are so many things to do and so little time. We are workaholics, pathological activists, activity addicts, people who cannot slow down even when our physical constitution violently protests against the pressures we impose upon it.

An increasing number of Americans have begun to understand this, and the popularity of such practices as Yoga, Transcendental Meditation, and the cultivation of alpha states indicate that many of us have realized that if we repress the Mary dimension of our selfhood, we are only half human; indeed, as Jesus says in the gospel today, it is the poorer half of humanity that is dominant. Action should be based on contemplation; contemplation should follow over into action if we are to have full, rich, authentic, well-developed personalities. The fully developed Christian, the follower of Jesus of Nazareth blends, as he did, Martha and Mary during all the hours of the day. The authentic human being does not switch back and forth from Martha to Mary; even in our most active moments there is a little bit of Mary and in our most contemplative moments we do not cut ourselves off from loving service to others. The goal of the Christian life is Martha-like service of other human beings with Mary-like contemplation adding depth, breadth, gentleness, love to that service.

We all know what it's like to take time off, to withdraw for a while from the demands of everyday life, to think, reflect, pray. Retreats and Days of Recollection are not as popular now as they used to be, and that is a misfortune because while many of them were not very good, the idea of time off for Blessed Solitude was an excellent one. Group discussions are fine, but they are no substitute for the peace, the quiet, the serenity, the calm of solitude. One comes away from such experiences with new energy, new vitality, new commitment and dedication. It is ironic that just as many non-Catholics are discovering the importance of meditation, Days of Recollection are less popular with Catholics than they used to be.

While it is certainly true that the ideal of Christian life is a mixture, a blending of Martha and Mary, we can only begin to strive toward that ideal when we impose on ourselves the rigid discipline required to stop being Martha all the time. Even those who are skilled at combining the Martha role and the Mary role still must take time off to concentrate principally on being Mary. The rest of us, who don't have much in the way of Mary skill at all, must begin by finding a little time each day, to pull away from the rush, the hurry of daily life and reflect on what life really means and who it is who has brought us into the world in order that we might return his love.

31

Now once he was in a certain place praying, and when he had finished one of his disciples said, "Lord, teach us to pray, just as John taught his disciples." He said to them, "Say this when you pray:

'Father, may your name be held holy,
your kingdom come;
give us each day our daily bread,
and forgive us our sins,
for we ourselves forgive each one who is in debt to us.
And do not put us to the test.' "

He also said to them, "Suppose one of you has a friend and goes to him in the middle of the night to say, 'My friend, lend me three loaves, because a friend of mine on his travels has just arrived at my house and I have nothing to offer him'; and the man answers from inside the house, 'Do not bother me. The door is bolted now, and my children and I are in bed; I cannot get up to give it to you.' I tell you, if the man does not get up and give it to him for friendship's sake, persistence will be enough to make him get up and give his friend all he wants.

"So I say to you: Ask, and it will be given to you; search, and you will find; knock, and the door will be opened to you. For the one who asks always receives; the one who searches always finds; the one who knocks will always have the door opened to him. What father among you would hand his son a stone when he asked for bread? Or hand him a snake instead of a fish? Or hand him a scorpion if he asked for an egg? If you then, who are evil,

*know how to give your children what is good, how much
more will the heavenly Father give the Holy Spirit to those
who ask him!"*

Luke 11:1-13

ADOLESCENCE, it is said, is a time when a young man
believes that he will never become as dumb as his father is.
If such an epigram is correct, then presumably adulthood
is the time when one discovers that one's father has learned
a lot in the last several years and is now not so dumb after
all. Childhood is the time when one thinks one's parents
know everything and can do everything. Disillusionment
about parents is part of growing from childhood to adolescence; rediscovery of parents is part of growing from
adolescence to adulthood. The theme of Luke's gospel is
that the authentic Christian adult is one who lives with
childlike trust in the heavenly Father. You become a
Christian adult when you rediscover, or discover for the
first time, that you can *really* trust God.

People who have carefully studied the scripture agree
that the passage we hear in this gospel is one of the most
important sections in all of the scripture. It is important
not merely because it provides us with one version of the
prayer we say every day (a shorter version, you will notice
—think of how much time you could save if you said the
shorter "Our Father" instead of the longer one!), but because it is the best and clearest evidence we have of the
relationship Jesus claimed to have with his Father in
heaven.

Most religions of the world and most religious leaders
have spoken of God as "the Father," but the English
translation, "Father," does not begin to convey what the

Hebrew word *Abba* really means. It is not a formal, respectful title of honor; it's a casual, informal, affectionate word that a little child might use toward an indulgent father who is bouncing him or her on his knee. *Abba* could better be translated, "Pop" or "Daddy" or "Daddy-o." Adults in the time of Jesus used the term of their earthly fathers, but only in intimate conversations and only at very special times. There is no record anywhere in all Hebraic literature—scripture or otherwise—of anyone ever being so bold, so presumptuous, so disrespectful as to call the Father in heaven by the affectionate term *Abba*. Those who heard Jesus use it must have been profoundly shocked, and the early Christians were also uneasy with the word, because when they translated it into Latin and Greek they used two much more solemn and respectful words. Who did Jesus think he was, daring to call the Lord of creation, the Alpha and the Omega, the Prime Mover, Being itself, the Ground of Being, by a name very much like "Pops" or, as the Irish would say the "Ould Fella"?

The answer is that Jesus presumed to address the heavenly Father so familiarly because he claimed a special relationship of intimacy with him, a relationship absolutely different, unique, and totally unheard of ever before in human history. Virtually all of our Christology, all of our thinking about the presence of divinity in Jesus can ultimately be traced to and grounded in this claim of special, affectionate relationship with the Father in heaven. But Jesus was not claiming such a relationship in order to exalt his own role or to find arguments for the theology books of the future. He was more interested in revealing something about God than in defining his own role. In calling God "Abba," he was saying in effect that the Ultimate is the sort of Being with whom one can enter friendly, intimate, casual, informal, relaxed, lovingly affectionate relationships. The Ground of Being, in other words, is a Thou.

More than that, Jesus told us that we too, can call him "Daddy-o" or "the Ould Fella" if we want. It is not blasphemous, not irreverent, not insulting; it's the kind of lovingly affectionate relationship that the heavenly Father wants. For Jesus, in teaching his followers the Lord's Prayer, told them that they, too, could dare to call the heavenly Father by the name "Abba"; they, too, could claim a relationship of affectionate intimacy with the maker of everyone and everything. Again, it was a profoundly shocking, a terribly scandalous, an outrageous suggestion. Christians have backed away from it ever since Jesus first taught the Lord's Prayer. It just doesn't seem right to think about God or to talk about him that way—not even if he himself insisted, through Jesus, that it is all right to do so. We know, in other words, what God wants better than God does!

The other side of the coin is that if we can be so lovingly affectionate with God, then we are justified in having the same trust in him that a child has in the father he calls "Da-da" or the mother he calls "Ma-ma." When we grow older we discover that our human mothers and fathers do not know everything and cannot do everything; they have their faults, limitations, imperfections just like everyone else. Still we have pleasant memories of the time when our mother and father were our whole world and we believed that nothing was impossible for them. They could make every hurt go away, they could gratify every need, they could respond to every love. Psychological adulthood requires us to realize that our parents are not omniscient, omnipotent; but religious adulthood, for the Christian at any rate, requires that we become so mature, so sophisticated, so brave that we can commit ourselves to trust and love and affection to our heavenly Father who does know everything and can do everything. He cares for us the way a doting father does for a little kid in his arms. It is a very brave and very wise person who can live that way.

How many times have we said the "Our Father" during our life? Do we really live like we believe that the Father in heaven can provide our daily bread and everything else we need? In the power of his affectionate love, are we really strong enough to forgive those who have offended us? Are we really ready to live lives of love and trust, affection and forgiveness?

32

A man in the crowd said to him, "Master, tell my brother to give me a share of our inheritance." "My friend," he replied, "who appointed me your judge, or the arbitrator of your claims?" Then he said to them, "Watch, and be on your guard against avarice of any kind, for a man's life is not made secure by what he owns, even when he has more than he needs."

Then he told them a parable: "There was once a rich man who, having had a good harvest from his land, thought to himself, 'What am I to do? I have not enough room to store my crops.' Then he said, 'This is what I will do: I will pull down my barns and build bigger ones, and store all my grain and my goods in them, and I will say to my soul: My soul, you have plenty of good things laid by for many years to come; take things easy, eat, drink, have a good time.' But God said to him, 'Fool! This very night the demand will be made for your soul; and this hoard of yours, whose will it be then?' So it is when a man stores up treasure for himself in place of making himself rich in the sight of God."

Luke 12:13-21

ONE of the most cheerless things we can do is to gather the few personal possessions of someone who has just been buried. The things that survive us after we have gone to the grave seem so pitiable and pathetic: An old purse, battered wallet, some books preserved for many years, pictures from childhood or the early years of marriage, a

141

handful of jewelry or cuff links, maybe an old transistor radio, clothes to be sent off to the Salvation Army or Catholic Charities; and then everything is gone. Nothing remains but memories.

What is the possession we prize most? Not our car or our house, but something that belongs just to us. Is it a collection of records, a camera, a set of finely bound books, a fur coat, some jewelry, a college or graduate school diploma? Is it antique furniture or something of very small monetary value which is important because of someone or something that recalls a special memory? Our father's watch, perhaps, or our mother's engagement ring? Let us ask ourselves where that possession will be in fifty years, and where we will be? Unless we are very young, we will be dead and buried, and the possession will probably vanish into a trash heap, or be stored away in a dusty attic, or buried under a pile of junk in an unattended corner of a basement. Perhaps it will belong to someone who never knew us and will never know or care what we were really like.

Consider an antique chair—an expensive one, perhaps one hundred and fifty years old. Who was the man who made it? Who bought it and used it first? What were their hopes, their dreams, their aspirations, their joys? What has happened to all these people and all the good things they wanted in their lives? They are gone, buried, most likely forgotten; yet the chair endures. We may think with regret once or twice about those who have enjoyed the lovely chair, and we shed a silent tear for ourselves because someday we too will be gone while the chair remains—an even more valuable antique to be admired by those who are as yet unborn.

And yet we work so hard, make so many sacrifices, plan so diligently, worry about so many things. What good does it all do? All human activities are vanity. How many of us know people who planned and saved for years, looking forward eagerly to the relaxation and enjoyment they would have at retirement? It came; they found it empty and hollow, and within a year they were dead. What purpose did it all serve? We may have built a big barn for ourselves, we may be as rich as J. Paul Getty and Howard Hughes combined; or we may have only a very little barn and be as rich as most people. When our bodies are lowered into the ground, it's all the same.

Does anything at all count in life? Can we store up any treasure that will survive? Many things indeed are vanity, but some things are not. Kindness, generosity, fidelity, trust, commitment, patience, sensitivity, cheerfulness, persistence, loyalty—all of these are possessions which we can store up in superabundance, and they never cease to exist. But a single act of kindness, a single promise kept, a harsh word suppressed have an impact on the human condition that can never be erased. This is true even in the strictly psychological and sociological order. We don't correct injustice in the world, of course, by being pleasant; we don't discharge our obligations to humankind by being patient. Still, a discharge of obligation that is done impatiently or a struggle for justice that is done self-righteously is foolish and counterproductive.

Jesus came to tell us that it is not merely that the treasures of noble, generous, graceful human actions improve the psychosocial environment in which we live; they are stored up (not, indeed, in a giant record book kept as the heavenly version of *The Guinness Book of Records*) and become part of the fierce struggle between good and evil that rages in the universe. They stand with Jesus and triumph with him in his resurrection and our ultimate victory over death. This struggle of life and death, good and

143

evil, began at the beginning and will go on till the end of humankind. We Christians, of course, believe that we personally survive; but we also believe that our actions, our efforts, our dedication and commitment are important. They are part of something that goes far beyond us and reaches from the Alpha to the Omega. And even if those who come after us may forget us, still the good things we have done will live forever, and so, too will we.

During the summer months we are supposed to slow down, although frequently our vacations are at least as hectic as the rest of the year. Still, during vacation time, it is good to ask how much energy are we putting into the foolish and frivolous task of building for ourselves a bigger barn?

33

"See that you are dressed for action and have your lamps lit. Be like men waiting for their master to return from the wedding feast, ready to open the door as soon as he comes and knocks. Happy those servants whom the master finds awake when he comes. I tell you solemnly, he will put on an apron, sit them down at table and wait on them. It may be in the second watch he comes, or in the third, but happy those servants if he finds them ready. You may be quite sure of this, that if the householder had known at what hour the burglar would come, he would not have let anyone break through the wall of his house. You too must stand ready, because the Son of Man is coming at an hour you do not expect."

Luke 12:35-40

VACATION time is the time when the boss is away. It doesn't matter who you are, every person has a boss. It is a rare situation in which the boss's departure is not greeted with a sigh of relief. For a couple of weeks, anyhow, everyone can relax.

When the boss leaves the office on vacation, when the foreman is away from the assembly line, when mother and father go out, when teacher leaves the classroom, when big brother or sister aren't looking, when there is no policeman on the highway, and, yes, if the truth be told, in many parishes when the pastor is away for a rest, then those who are left behind relax just a little bit (sometimes more than a little bit). When there is little chance of sanction being imposed, then one may cut corners. It's not that important things don't get done, but we are more relaxed and casual about the way we do them and about how long it takes. The worst thing that can happen is to have the absent one return early or without warning. The boss, the cop on the beat, mom and dad, mother superior, the foreman, teacher—all occasionally display a disconcerting ability to reappear much too early—unannounced and without warning.

The Boy Scout motto, "Be prepared," may be a cliche, but it is also sound advice. Nevertheless, we don't always follow it, and all of us have been caught with a hand in the cookie jar at one time or other. It is surely the case that no matter how long we live or however much warning we have, death will come too suddenly and catch us unprepared. For some people, it will come early in life with the screech of brakes and the crash of metal against metal; for others it will come unexpectedly in the middle years when a hydraulic system fails on a jet; with the flash of a knife blade on a dark city street; from the treacherous multiplication of white cells in leukemia; with the sudden failure of the life-pumping heart muscle. Even if we die at an advanced age of a lingering illness we are still not ready, we are still not prepared. God will still come for us at the wrong time. He came back too soon; we didn't quite have enough time to get everything organized to go off with him.

But it would be a mistake to think of God's coming for us only in the final moments of our lives. The Lord walks by us every day, passes us in the street, rides up and down the elevator with us, walks into the classroom, drives by in the car, sits down at the table to eat with us. He is present every day in all the opportunities, challenges, and invitations that he issues to us through his brothers and sisters who are our friends, our families, our co-workers and the strangers who come down our paths. But we are so busy about so many things, there are so many different cookie jars with our hands in them, so many things to be done while God isn't looking that we don't notice him sitting across the table from us, or walking down the corridor, or asking us questions, or coming to us for help. We are too weighed down with problems, opportunities, responsibilities, anxieties, fears, cares, worries, ambitions, desires, discouragements to know that the Lord is there with us, that he has already returned. He will not come tomorrow or the next day or five years from now; he is present at this moment, waiting expectantly to see how we will act now that he has arrived on the scene. A local angel might just pass by and whisper in our ear, "Jiggers, the boss is back!"

The two comings of the Lord are not unrelated, of course. For if we lived everyday realizing that "the boss is back," then when he does come for the final time, we will be as ready as any human being can be. If we are not surprised to discover him around the corner, down the hall, in the house next door, today, then neither will be surprised when he comes to bring us home for good. The old spiritual adage that we ought to live each day as though it were the last may have been sound advice, but only the great saints could follow it in practice, and sometimes one suspects that even they couldn't. After a while it just becomes psychologically impossible to persuade oneself that realistically today just might be the last day of our life. Of course, it could be, but the odds are heavily against it. However, there is wisdom in the old adage, because even if it is the last day of our lives, the best way to prepare, indeed the only way to prepare, is to continue to serve the Lord and his brothers and sisters who are around us. If we do our best to see him in the opportunities he offers us in our fellow human beings each day of our lives, then we are indeed living each day as if it were our last.

How did the Lord come to us yesterday? Where did we encounter him? How did he catch us by surprise? Did we miss him completely? Where are we likely to see him today?

34

Through towns and villages he went teaching, making his way to Jerusalem. Someone said to him, "Sir, will there be only a few saved?" He said to them, "Try your best to enter by a narrow door, because, I tell you, many will try to enter and will not succeed.

"Once the master of the house has got up and locked the door, you may find yourself knocking on the door, saying, 'Lord, open to us' but he will answer, 'I do not know where you come from.' Then you will find yourself saying, 'We once ate and drank in your company; you taught in our streets' but he will reply, 'I do not know where you come from. Away from me, all you wicked men!

"Then there will be weeping and grinding of teeth, when you see Abraham and Isaac and Jacob and all the prophets in the kingdom of God, and yourselves turned outside. And men from east and west, from north and south, will come to take their places at the feast in the kingdom of God.

"Yes, there are those now last who will be first, and those now first who will be last."

Luke 13:22-30

THINK of what America would be like if we did not have Mexican and Italian food, black music, Jewish humor, Irish politics and poetry. Polish warmth and enthusiasm, Hispanic mysticism. Think of what life would be like if children and adults led completely segregated existences. Think of what adult life would be like if you were only permitted to associate with those who were your own age. Think of how dull the year would be if there were no changes in the seasons. A homogenized world is a dull and bland world. "Variety is the spice of life" is more than just a cliche; it is profound wisdom.

But there are times when the spice turns into poison. Think of the ethnic and racial conflicts in our big cities, the generational conflict between parents and children, the struggle between the older and the younger in almost any human organization and community, the endless conflicts which weaken the love of husband and wife. Differences may be fabulous, but they are also fatiguing; they may be wonderful, but they are also wearisome; they may be glorious, but oftentimes they seem intolerably grim. God puts too much spice into life.

Variety, then, brings both spice and agony to life. If we understand that, we can grasp the curious paradox in the two outrageous sayings of Jesus in today's gospel. On the one hand, he tells us that it is as difficult to get into heaven as it is to get through a very narrow door (the eye of the needle?), and on the other hand, he tells us that people are going to pour in from all the corners of the earth. Once more, Jesus is engaging in an almost impossible rhetoric. He defies us to take him literally and not to be shaken and troubled by the magic he works with words. Responding to the heavenly Father's invitation is both difficult and easy, difficult because it takes so much courage and faith, easy because it appeals to the depths of the human heart no matter in what part of the world.

It is a mistake to try to explain or to explain away the startling combination of images in today's gospel. Jesus is trying to astonish, trying to shock us, trying to make us think. But without explaining away the paradox, and without trying to deprive the words of Jesus of their electric excitement, we can still see that the two sayings are not inconsistent. One of the great burdens of human life is putting up with those who are different from us. By opening up the Kingdom of Heaven to all humans, Jesus made it both attractive to everyone and difficult for everyone—attractive because his gospel appeals to all human beings and difficult because we have to put up with them. It was good of Jesus to invite us, but why did he have to invite all these other strange and peculiar people? Why is there room for *them* in the Kingdom of Heaven?

So, paradoxically, by making it easy for us, Jesus also makes it difficult, because that which is easy for us is easy for others; and the others make things difficult by daring to be different from us. (To make matters worse, they are offended because we are different from them.) There isn't any choice about it. In a diversified world, a religion which is catholic—that is, *for* everyone—is also going to be troublesome *to* everyone. Once you start letting in people of different races, languages, nationalities, and cultural backgrounds, then you create problems. Then *we* have to put up with *them*.

And there are, unfortunately, only two ways to react to them. We can fight them, because they dare to be different, or we can enjoy them, because their difference is exciting, interesting, rewarding, fascinating. All those other folk who are jammed into our church with us can either be spice or agony for life. Generally, of course, they are a little bit of both. Since they will not go away and since Jesus seems to like his church variegated, the best thing to do is to learn how to put up with those who are different from us and then begin to enjoy them. But, as we well know from tolerating people of different language, culture, race, age or sex, enjoying those who are different from us—though it ought to be easy—is a very, very difficult task. It is indeed like getting through a very narrow door after we've had too much to eat.

In this gospel Jesus is attacking complacency. Complacent persons think that they have done enough, that nothing more is required of them; by honoring the rules and belonging to the right group of people, they have sewn up everything and solved all their problems. Jesus is telling us that salvation is not that easy. Belonging to a people or a church and keeping a certain set of rules (however strict and lofty) is much easier than living a life of faith and love—a life of enthusiasm, commitment, and joy. It is expected that those who respond to the invitation to the heavenly Father's wedding banquet will put forth unending effort. We are confident that we can sustain this effort with the help of the heavenly Father, but we permit ourselves no illusions that the effort can be dispensed with.

There are really two kinds of people when it comes to prejudice toward diversity: those who acknowledge their prejudices and those who do not. Human beings who claim that they have no spontaneous reactions of suspicion, distrust, or dislike when they encounter diversity are kidding either themselves or us or both. If we are wise, we acknowledge our spontaneous reactions of prejudice and then try to transcend them, so that dislike turns into enjoyment. It would be wise, then, for each of us to make a list of those groups of humans we dislike the most and then, after each group, record (mentally at least) that which is most enjoyable about them. If we cannot find anything enjoyable, then the door is very narrow indeed.

35

From that time Jesus began to make it clear to his disciples that he was destined to go to Jerusalem and suffer griev- ously at the hands of the elders and chief priests and scribes, to be put to death and to be raised up on the third day. Then, taking him aside, Peter started to remonstrate with him. "Heaven preserve you, Lord"; he said "this must not happen to you." But he turned and said to Peter, "Get behind me, Satan! You are an obstacle in my path, be- cause the way you think is not God's way but man's."

Then Jesus said to his disciples, "If anyone wants to be a follower of mine, let him renounce himself and take up his cross and follow me. For anyone who wants to save his life will lose it; but anyone who loses his life for my sake will find it. What, then, will a man gain if he wins the whole world and ruins his life? Or what has a man to offer in exchange for his life?

"For the Son of Man is going to come in the glory of his Father with his angels, and when he does, he will reward each one according to his behavior."

Matthew 16:21-27

FEW human experiences are more unpleasant than being ridiculed. Our faces flush, our lips press together. We may laugh because we have no choice, but we are still angry. We wish we could vanish from the face of the earth or that we could strike a savage blow to destroy our cruel tormen- tors. Some ridicule is harmless and affectionate, but a good deal of what passes for affectionate and friendly ridicule is nasty and destructive. Ridicule is an effective means of controlling children and old people, the weak and the powerless, as well as the strong and the successful. Ridiculing another person is one of the cruelest things we can do.

There has been a lot of needless ridicule in the post-Vatican Council church. Old forms of piety, old devotions, old religious practices are made fun of, despite the fact that many people shaped their whole religious lives around these old forms. Devotion to the Sacred Heart, the Sorrowful Mother Novenas, even the rosarian devotion to Mary have been laughed at by many young and not-so-young people who think they know all the answers. Those who had large families because they thought that is what the church wanted them to do now find themselves the objects of scorn from many of those who have a different, more "modern" version of what Catholicism expects from its people. People who have committed their lives to one kind of ministry discover that that ministry is now irrelevant, and teachers who thought that teaching in Catholic schools was the best thing they could do with their lives find, as life comes to an end, that Catholic schools are no longer "the answer."

The point is not that the church shouldn't change; the church must change, at least in those things that are not essential, in order to respond more effectively to the needs of its people. Nor is the point that single-minded enthusiasts should not harass those who were born a couple of decades earlier. (They should not, of course, but the single-minded enthusiasts we will always have with us.) The point is that the person who takes his or her religion seriously is going to be derided by those who are not Christians but also by those who are members of the household of the faith, and in some cases even by those who are or claim to be serious and dedicated. Not only will your enemies go after you, in other words, but even those who purport to be your friends—and in some cases even those who can lay some legitimate claim to being your friends—will go after you. Dedicated commitment, as Jesus points out vigorously in today's gospel, means losing one's life to find it—taking up a cross, dying, and being buried in order to be born again.

Those who are serious about anything run the risk of having to "lose their life" by being ridiculed. Those who work hard are ridiculed by those who loaf; those who take precautions with their health are ridiculed by those who do not ("There you go, jogging again! You sure do look silly.") Those who carefully supervise their children are made fun of by those who couldn't be bothered; those who work hard at both the positive and negative demands of marital fidelity are scorned by those who take marriage obligations lightly; and at the end of your life, what do you have to show for it? Your hard work has not made all that much difference, your marriage had its ups and downs, you're going to die anyway, and your children didn't turn out to be the paragons you'd hoped they would be. All your hard work, your dedication, your seriousness, your commitment seem to have been wasted.

To be ridiculed, then, is merely part of the risk—maybe the lesser part—of serious commitment. For serious commitments to church, spouse, family, the responsibilities of life, at best work out only moderately well and often seem to end up flawed failures. You have given your life, you have dedicated your life, you have, in the words of the invitation of Jesus, "lost your life"; and there doesn't seem to be any particular hope of finding it.

The Gospel is aimed at the frustration and failures of life, of which ridicule is only one sharply painful aspect.

It would seem that all Jesus can offer us is an invitation to serious commitment, on the one hand, and a promise that our commitment will lead to a loss of life, on the other hand, through failure, frustration, discouragement, disillusionment, weariness. Jesus does not promise that we will escape any of these things. On the contrary, he seems to guarantee that we will not escape them; he contents himself with the invitation to take up your losses and follow after him. We must plod on even though frustrated, keep on trying even though derided, work hard even though discouraged, drag along our cross even though the effort seems worthless; for it is precisely by doing such unromantic and monotonous things that we will find our lives, that we will live again, that we will learn to live forever.

36

Great crowds accompanied him on his way and he turned and spoke to them. "If any man comes to me without hating his father, mother, wife, children, brothers, sisters, yes and his own life too, he cannot be my disciple. Anyone who does not carry his cross and come after me cannot be my disciple.

"And indeed, which of you here, intending to build a tower, would not first sit down and work out the cost to see if he had enough to complete it? Otherwise, if he laid the foundation and then found himself unable to finish the work, the onlookers would all start making fun of him and saying, 'Here is a man who started to build and was unable to finish.' Or again, what king marching to war against another king would not first sit down and consider whether with ten thousand men he could stand up to the other who advanced against him with twenty thousand? If not, then while the other king was still a long way off, he would send envoys to sue for peace. So in the same way, none of you can be my disciple unless he gives up all his possessions."

Luke 14:25-33

THE quintessential ending of a western movie has the hero riding out of town over the hills into the sunset while everyone waves a sad farewell to him. Shane goes over the mountain while the little boy Shane leaves cries for him to return. The cowpoke does not want to leave. The comforts of a possible home and family and close friends are

157

attractive. But much more compelling—even demanding—are the requirements of his own integrity, his own commitment, his own obligation to follow where his true self leads him. He is not even sure exactly where that may be, but he knows that he must go on further west over the mountain—to the next town, to the next adventure. Shane, riding away from home and family, is the perfect example of what Jesus means in this gospel. He does not "hate" the lovely widow and her son as we would normally use the word. On the contrary, he loves them very much. But there is a higher calling, a higher mission, a higher destiny for Shane, and he loves that even more than he loves his good friends whom he must leave behind.

Luke's gospel is concerned with commitment. The first part depicts the kind of commitment demanded of the followers of Jesus. And in the parables in the second part of the gospel Jesus warns us against hasty commitments that are not thought through. "Do not choose to follow me," he says, "unless you really know what you're doing. Make no shallow or superficial commitments to be my disciples until you have thought out well the implications. Because if you have not understood the full demands that I make on my followers and you follow for shallow or silly or superficial reasons, then you are going to make a fool out of yourself just as did the King who went into battle without considering the size of the enemy's army, or the man who tried to build a fortress and was not able to finish it because he didn't have the money for the materials and labor he needed to complete the tower." Know what you're getting into, Jesus says, or you will look singularly foolish.

Someone goes blithely off to medical school or law school without realizing how much study is required and then comes home in disgrace because he/she just didn't feel like studying. Someone travels to another part of the country to take a new job and comes back after a few weeks saying he simply didn't like that part of the country. Someone builds a home in a new neighborhood and then in a short period of time puts it up on the market saying the people in the neighborhood aren't friendly. In each instance we wonder why someone dashes into a new venture without checking things out first. Why didn't the student find out how hard law or medical school would be? Why didn't the fellow with the new job visit Alaska first before he decided it was a great place to live? Why didn't you talk to the people in the new neighborhood before you determined that was the place you wanted to build your big new house? Marry in haste, repent at leisure, the old saying goes. Make an impulsive decision and then look awfully foolish when you have to back out.

It is a very hard-nosed position that Jesus takes in the gospel today; one of the most hard-nosed statements in the whole New Testament. Obviously Jesus wants all of us to be his followers, but he does not want us to climb on his band wagon, to sign on his ship, to join his team with any illusion. If you want to be a follower of mine, Jesus says, fine; but don't come in haste because having proclaimed yourself a Christian you're going to look awfully foolish when you try to back out. And don't kid yourself into thinking it's going to be a very easy commitment to honor, for I demand of you your whole life. You must be ready to trust me and the goodness I preach more than you trust your family or any other factor or influence in your world. That's what you're getting into; and if you don't like it, then don't get into it in the first place.

It's a practical, realistic, even somewhat cynical business but we should have no doubts at all that Jesus meant exactly what he said. If we believe the good news of his heavenly Father's loving graciousness which he has revealed to us, if we really believe the world is animated by passionate love, if we really believe that all our brightest

159

dreams can and have come true, then we'd better be prepared to live according to such beliefs and to make the sacrifices required for such a life. There are rewards, of course. We will lead happier, richer, fuller, more generous, more productive and creative lives. We will have to surrender our trust completely to God and to Jesus and no one —even our nearest and most beloved—can be permitted to interfere with the service of Jesus and the heavenly Father.

In fact, those who follow Jesus have the strength and the vigor and the courage to be even closer and warmer in their love of their families than those who do not. They have more to give and more reason to be generous. The point of the gospel is not that we should turn away from our families but that the influence of God as revealed to us in Jesus ought to be even stronger and more powerful in our lives than the influence of our families. This is not poetic exaggeration, this is not pretty rhetoric; this is the blunt statement of the way things are. If our families and our friends are depressed, pessimistic, or unhappy, then our faith must be stronger than their influence. We must be joyous, cheerful, and happy because that is what is demanded of those who follow Jesus.

Jesus is telling us, in effect, that before we commit ourselves to lives of joy, and happiness, and courage, and risk-taking we should know exactly what we are getting into. Don't take a ride on a wild roller coaster before you've got some idea what the bumps and the twists and the turns are. The lives of Jesus' followers are on a roller coaster— exciting, unpredictable, exhilarating and scary. We should ask ourselves today whether we are brave enough to take the risk of getting on that roller coaster. We should ask ourselves today whether we are brave enough to pay the costs of such a ride.

37

Then Peter went up to him and said, "Lord, how often must I forgive my brother if he wrongs me? As often as seven times?" Jesus answered, "Not seven, I tell you, but seventy-seven times.

"And so the kingdom of heaven may be compared to a king who decided to settle his accounts with his servants. When the reckoning began, they brought him a man who owed ten thousand talents; but he had no means of payment, so his master gave orders that he should be sold, together with his wife and children and all his possessions, to meet the debt. At this, the servant threw himself down at his master's feet. 'Give me time' he said 'and I will pay the whole sum.' And the servant's master felt so sorry for him that he let him go and cancelled the debt. Now as this servant went out, he happened to meet a fellow servant who owed him one hundred denarii; and he seized him by the throat and began to throttle him. 'Pay what you owe me' he said. His fellow servant fell at his feet and implored him, saying, 'Give me time and I will pay you.' But the other would not agree; on the contrary, he had him thrown into prison till he should pay the debt. His fellow servants were deeply distressed when they saw what had happened, and they went to their master and reported the whole affair to him. Then the master sent for him. 'You wicked servant,' he said 'I cancelled all that debt of yours when you appealed to me. Were you not bound, then, to have pity on your fellow servant just as I had pity on you?' And in his anger the master handed him over to the torturers till he should pay all his debt. And that is how my heavenly

FIFTY-TWO GOSPEL MEDITATIONS

Father will deal with you unless you each forgive your brother from your heart."

Matthew 18:21-35

MOST married people who have a happy and growing relationship will tell you, perhaps confidentially and off the record, that the secret of a successful marriage is learning how to fight. They may have been given pious advice in their families or in their schools or in pre-Cana conferences that people who love each other should not fight; but in the real world of daily living together, what counts is not avoiding conflict but knowing how to carry on the conflict. Indeed, those couples who claim they never fight may have a very happy marriage, but they may also be repressing dangerous tensions and conflicts. In that terrible, saccharine movie *Love Story* we were informed that "Love means never having to say you're sorry." In truth, however, love means being able to say "I'm sorry." Matthew's gospel is about mercy and forgiveness, which is to say it is about love, love operating in conflict situations.

We have all experienced conflict with those whom we love—our parents, children, close friends, colleagues, our spouse. At the height of the conflict there is always a strong urge in the personality that says, silently if not aloud, "Getting involved with someone like you was a terrible mistake. The best thing I could do would be to get uninvolved just as quickly as possible." Then comes mercy, forgiveness, reconciliation; and we look back on that urge to escape the one we love and can scarcely believe we thought that way. Love grows not so much through a peaceful, untroubled path by which one slowly climbs the gentle slope of an ancient mountain but rather through a series of wild, desperate leaps—over rocks, across chasms, along treacherous crevasses. Each new leap almost always involves mercy, forgiveness and reconciliation.

Let us leave aside for the moment that question of forgiveness of the enemy who is not intimate with us. Reconciliation, of course, is desirable in such conflicts too, though it might not be possible in some instances (forgiveness in the depths of one's heart is always possible, of course). Far more important for most of us in our ordinary daily lives is not so much the forgiveness of the distant enemy but of the intimate enemy, the enemy who is also the beloved.

The mercy the king demands of his servant in the gospel is absolutely essential in any close human relationship. For a human relationship in which it is necessary for one of the partners always to be right and the other to be always wrong is a very unhealthy relationship. The reconciliation dialogue is always one in which one partner asks for forgiveness and the other shows mercy. We have in such a dialogue a situation just like the one described by Jesus in the gospel. The wicked servant cheerfully accepts God's mercy but won't show mercy to others. We cannot say "I'm sorry" to God unless we're willing to say it to our fellow human beings, particularly the intimate enemy. A human relationship that gets so badly stylized that one person is permanently dispensed from saying "I'm sorry," while the other person is also permanently dispensed from responding mercifully, is unbalanced and possibly in serious trouble.

The difference between the king and the wicked servant in the gospel story is that the servant kept very careful account books and the king did not. The king did not store up injury, mispayments or past wrongs, biding his time for the marvelous day when he could dump all the stored-up injuries on the servant's head. He was ready to wipe the slate clean, forget about the past and start anew. But the wicked servant was a careful accountant and kept very detailed books. He stored up all the memories of past mispayments and demanded payment in full. So it is with us. Not only should we forgive, we also have to forget, at least to the extent of wiping the slate clean, canceling the record in the account books, and resolutely refusing to hold grudges. The king in today's gospel did not bear grudges; the wicked servant did. Are we the kind to bear grudges, or are we like the king, ready to wipe the slate clean, and begin again?

Oftentimes those intimate relationships in which there is no conflict mask a variety of suppressed grudges, a lot of reckoning, of cooly waiting for the opportunity to settle the score and get even. Much better that people fight than wait for the day of reckoning. But how do you go about fighting? There are enormous differences in personality styles. It is important to be aware of these differences and to realize that no one approach is necessarily superior to the other. In close human relationships, particularly marriage, people must be very sensitive to their partner's style of processing conflict, fighting, mercy, reconciliation. Both partners must be willing to adjust their own style to the other's style. If the styles are drastically different, neither partner can legitimately claim that his or her style of processing conflict is the only correct one. Otherwise one gets into the vicious circle of fighting about how to fight, conflicting about how to have conflicts, and refusing to exercise mercy about the way mercy is to be bestowed. In such intimate relationship the protocols and the processes have to be worked out, compromises must be made, solutions that everybody can live with must be realized. But just as it will simply not do for one person to have the monopoly of granting mercy and the other the monopoly on the obligation to seek forgiveness, so it will not do at all in a mature human relationship for one person to impose his or her own particular style of conflict and reconciliation on the other.

How do you process conflict with your intimate enemies? Is your style more that of the king or that of the wicked servant? Do you insist that you be the one to give forgiveness, never the one to ask for it? Do you impose your mode of conflict on others whether they like it or not? Is now the time for you and your intimate enemy, who is also your beloved, to take a good, hard look at how you fight with one another and hence grow in love?

38

After leaving that place they made their way through Galilee; and he did not want anyone to know, because he was instructing his disciples; he was telling them, "The Son of Man will be delivered into the hands of men; they will put him to death; and three days after he has been put to death he will rise again." But they did not understand what he said and were afraid to ask him.

They came to Capernaum, and when he was in the house he asked them, "What were you arguing about on the road?" They said nothing because they had been arguing which of them was the greatest. So he sat down, called the Twelve to him and said, "If anyone wants to be first, he must make himself last of all and servant of all." He then took a little child, set him in front of them, put his arms around him, and said to them, "Anyone who welcomes one of these little children in my name, welcomes me; and anyone who welcomes me welcomes not me but the one who sent me."

Mark 9:30-37

COURTESY seems to have become a casualty of modern urban life. It still survives, perhaps, in parts of the South and the West and in small towns; in most big cities, however, one seldom hears such words as "please," "thank you," "you're welcome," and "pardon me." Indeed, you often get the impression that those who are being paid to do things for you have to exercise major restraints not to be systematically rude—and sometimes the restraints fail.

166

You pay your money and you get your ticket, your hamburger, your newspaper, the candy bar, the milk shake, the new car. You should be happy they're ready to sell the things to you; what reason do you have to expect courtesy too? One may hear lots of ads about "friendly skies" or courteous service station attendants, but after a while one learns they are a substitute for rather than a reflection of anything that is actually going to happen. The metallic courtesy of the voice on the public address system thanking you and asking you to come again might just as well be spoken by a computer; indeed, sometimes it sounds like it is. Service with a smile? You've got to be kidding!

This gospel deals with service. Mark tells us that the Messiah was also a Suffering Servant, a notion that seems almost to be a contradiction in terms to those who had first heard it. But here, in the gospel, Jesus, the expected one of the nations, insists on the obligation to be a servant and takes time out to be gracious and friendly with a little child. So little kids are pleasant and attractive at a distance or for about five minutes, but as anyone knows who has to put up with children for a long period of time, they can (and usually do) try the patience of a saint. Note well what Jesus says. It's not the familiar story about becoming like little children; the point is rather different. Those who follow Jesus, those who wish to imitate his service must also serve cheerfully, as he served the children. That is, as anyone who has children knows, asking an awful lot; it may be one of the reasons so many young people today seem reluctant to become parents at all. We don't keep the secret anymore that children, as fun and enjoyable as they can be, as attractive and charming as they often are, also are a tremendous burden, a horrendous obligation, an endless drag, and frequently a noisy nuisance. Do we love them? Of course, but there is also a great temptation

167

to break their little necks. The difference between the child abuser and the rest of us is simply that we have better control over our impulses, not that the impulses are any different. Jesus wants us to serve little children cheerfully, patiently, joyously all the time? He's got to be kidding.

We are tempted to say that if this is what Jesus had in mind, he really does expect us to be suffering servants, because anyone who has to serve and take care of little children does a lot of suffering—and it's even harder if you're expected to be cheerful and happy about it. Still there isn't much doubt that that is exactly what the gospel says. We must serve little children as though we were serving Jesus. That's a terribly high standard of service. If we must be patient and cheerful, kind and gentle with little children, what must we be like with adults?

The problem with courteous service, be it of kids or grownups, is that it requires patience. If there is more courtesy in the West and the South and in small towns, the reason may be that the pace of life is still slower there than it is in big cities in the rest of the country. Children make endless demands of us; they try our patience to the breaking point; so too, those of us who deal with the public everyday lose our patience because the public makes constant, hurried, impatient demands on us. An impatient public leads to impatient service, and impatient service (and most all of us serve others, if only members of our families) make for an impatient public. We are caught in a vicious circle of hurry, hassle and harass; too much to do and not enough time to do it. When the bills are paid, the food's on the table, the laundry done, the job completed, we have gotten through another day. Isn't that enough service? Jesus expects us to be patient and cheerful besides? He expects us not to lose our temper when someone complains about "ring around the collar" or says "when are we going to put the storm windows in?" He's got to be kidding.

So most of us don't have to go very far to find the cross we will carry after Jesus. It's right there waiting for us when we get out of bed in the morning. It's the obligation of putting up with other people and doing it cheerfully and willingly as gracious servants every day of our lives. The French philosopher Jean Paul Sartre said quite accurately that hell is other people. Well, maybe a Christian can't go quite that far, but purgatory certainly could be other people. The point Jesus makes in this gospel is that heaven is made up of other people too, or, more precisely and specifically, we get to heaven by serving other people. Resurrection is achieved through service, through service to little people, big people, nice people and not nice people, those we love, those we can't stand, those about whom we have mixed emotions.

Since just being human involves service and suffering, the question is not whether we serve but how. Do we follow Jesus' way and achieve resurrection by transcending the awful burdens of our own short temper and impatience, or do we serve with the grim determination of self-appointed martyrs, the rudeness of spiteful hirelings, the indifference of those who long ago gave up caring. Resurrection, it turns out, is something that begins in this life. He who can be the cheerful and patient servant has already begun his own resurrection. Oddly enough, because he doesn't complain he has already become happier.

Who is it in our life that makes the most difficult demands on our service? How are we doing at being cheerful and patient with that person? Are we really and truly prepared to think of that other as Jesus in our midst, and if we are not, can we really claim to be followers of Jesus?

39

"There was a rich man who used to dress in purple and fine linen and feast magnificently every day. And at his gate there lay a poor man called Lazarus, covered with sores, who longed to fill himself with the scraps that fell from the rich man's table. Dogs even came and licked his sores. Now the poor man died and was carried away by the angels to the bosom of Abraham. The rich man also died and was buried.

"In his torment in Hades he looked up and saw Abraham a long way off with Lazarus in his bosom. So he cried out, 'Father Abraham, pity me and send Lazarus to dip the tip of his finger in water and cool my tongue, for I am in agony in these flames.' 'My son,' Abraham replied 'remember that during your life good things came your way, just as bad things came the way of Lazarus. Now he is being comforted here while you are in agony. But that is not all: between us and you a great gulf has been fixed, to stop anyone, if he wanted to, crossing from our side to yours, and to stop any crossing from your side to ours.'

"The rich man replied, 'Father, I beg you then to send Lazarus to my father's house, since I have five brothers, to give them warning so that they do not come to this place of torment too.' 'They have Moses and the prophets,' said Abraham 'let them listen to them.' 'Ah no, father Abraham,' said the rich man 'but if someone comes to them from the dead, they will repent.' Then Abraham said to him, 'If they will not listen either to Moses or to the prophets, they will not be convinced even if someone should rise from the dead.'"

Luke 16:19-31

ONE of our problems in understanding the parables of Jesus is that it takes some imagination and skill to put ourselves into the situation in which Jesus was speaking. Often-times the writers of the gospels, who had other concerns than ours, are not a very great help to us in the exercise of our imagination. So unless there is someone around to interpret the scripture for us, we are often baffled. This gospel is a good case in point. Let us imagine that we are there, listening to Jesus talk.

His audience is impressed with the authority of his preaching, the depth of his wisdom, and the beauty of the Good News he brings; but they want *proof,* they want evidence, they want a miracle, a big, "supersign" from heaven to confirm that Jesus knows what he is talking about, that he is not a fraud, a madman, a charlatan. "You want a miracle? You know it wouldn't make any difference if you had one," says Jesus. "You still wouldn't believe. Take the story of Dives and Lazarus. . . ." And then Jesus tells them a story with which they are very familiar; but he puts a twist at the end for which they were quite unprepared. It is precisely this twist at the end that shatters their preconceptions, shakes their complacency, challenges them to a leap of faith. It is a characteristic preaching "trick" of Jesus, and unless we understand this preaching style, it is hard to appreciate the full richness of his parables.

So Jesus didn't have anything in mind in his homily about life after death (he dealt with that elsewhere). Nor in the original parable, at any rate, was Jesus saying anything about wealth and poverty (he dealt with that elsewhere). Rather, he took a story with which all his audience was familiar, a parable that all the other rabbis had used, and gave it a special twist at the end. The subject of the parable, in other words, was not survival, not wealth, but faith. If you don't believe the scripture, said Jesus, then you wouldn't even believe someone coming back from the dead. He had turned the tables once more on those who were trying to trap him. You have the Good News in the scripture of God's love, he said, you don't need science. If you believe the scriptures then you won't believe science. Faith is not caused by miracles, faith is caused by a leap of trust in God's loving goodness.

Oftentimes we wish we could be absolutely certain we will survive after death. Perhaps we even look to this parable for some hints about our survival. If only someone would come back from the dead, if only the Blessed Mother would appear to us, if only Jesus himself would appear, if only there was an absolutely convincing proof. Why doesn't Jesus provide for us an argument so strong that nothing could shake it.

The answer is clear in the gospel. If we do not believe the longings in our heart, if we do not believe God's love as it is revealed in the world all around us and revealed especially in the scriptures and in the preaching of Jesus, then someone could come back from the dead and we wouldn't believe that either. A perfectly convincing argument could be made for "life after death," and if we cannot believe the proof of a sunset, or a cool summer breeze or the smile of a child, or laughter on a spring day or the touch of a friendly hand, then we won't believe the most convincing philosophical or mathematical argument. The cynicism that makes us hesitate to believe that life is worth living, that there is purpose, that there is dignity, that there is happiness in the universe will not let us believe it even if someone came back from the dead, or if Jesus appeared in a cloud over our city or town at high noon. We worry because we want to worry. It is better to live in fear and cynicism than to live in hope and joy. No miracle, no sign from heaven, no perfect proof, no return visitor from the dead will change our minds if cynicism is that important.

Let us imagine ourselves, once again, there in the marketplace or at the side of the lake while Jesus is telling the story of Lazarus and Dives, giving it a twist at the end to catch us off balance. We are inclined to say, "You're wrong, Jesus. If somebody really did come back from the dead, then we'd really believe, wouldn't we?" Or is our quest for absolute certainty in fact the result of fear of taking risks and of committing ourselves to a God who claims to love us, and claims, furthermore, to have given us more than enough evidence to back it up.

40

Some Pharisees approached him and asked, "Is it against the law for a man to divorce his wife?" They were testing him. He answered them, "What did Moses command you?" "Moses allowed us" they said "to draw up a writ of dismissal and so to divorce." Then Jesus said to them, "It was because you were so unteachable that he wrote this commandment for you. But from the beginning of creation God made them male and female. This is why a man must leave father and mother, and the two become one body. They are no longer two, therefore, but one body. So then, what God has united, man must not divide." Back in the house the disciples questioned him again about this, and he said to them, "The man who divorces his wife and marries another is guilty of adultery against her. And if a woman divorces her husband and marries another she is guilty of adultery too."

People were bringing little children to him, for him to touch them. The disciples turned them away, but when Jesus saw this he was indignant and said to them, "Let the little children come to me; do not stop them; for it is to such as these that the kingdom of God belongs. I tell you solemnly, anyone who does not welcome the kingdom of God like a little child will never enter it." Then he put his arms around them, laid his hands on them and gave them his blessing.

Mark 10:2-16

IT is now estimated by the sober statisticians of the Bureau of the Census that between one out of four and one out of three American marriages are going to end in divorce. Furthermore, two out of three second marriages will end in divorce despite what we sometimes hear to the contrary that second marriages are less likely than first marriages to stay out of the divorce courts. Also, there seems to be an increasing number of women who are initiating divorce proceedings because they wish to escape from the responsibilities of being a wife and mother. Finally, the number of people not getting married seems to be increasing, and young people especially are often reluctant to make the definitive commitment to marriage and parenthood—even though in some cases they have no objection to living with someone indefinitely. The family, it would seem, is in a state of crisis and the future of marriage is in doubt.

But not, it turns out in all that much doubt. Most people still marry, however cautious they may have become about it, and most of those who marry continue married, while most of those who do divorce are not prevented by one unhappy experience from trying again. And however reluctant young people are to have children, they seem to love them once they appear on the scene, as intensely as anyone ever has. Finally, the so called alternative styles, such as "open marriage," "swinging singles," or similar things we read about in the Sunday paper are limited to a very small minority of most unhappy people. Though there is doubtless a crisis in marriage today, it is not one that suggests the family will go out of business. Despite all its weaknesses and imperfections, the family is still the most efficient way humankind has developed for releasing emotional energy, satisfying passion, and raising children. The logistical and organizational difficulties involved in all alternatives seem to make them impractical at best and destructive at worst.

An interesting example is to be found in recent research on the kibbutz in Israel. A strongly idealistic, highly motivated endeavor in human living, the kibbutz began as an experiment in communal property, communal work, and communal childrearing. The husband and wife relationship persisted (unlike some other communal experiments, there were not in the kibbutz communal sexual rights) but the entire community assumed responsibility for childrearing. The children spent only a small period each day with their biological parents, and except for the very early years even slept in dormitories at night. However, recent research indicates that the powerful trend of the kibbutz is back to the traditional family. Family life is flourishing in the kibbutz and growing ever stronger. The kibbutz experience shows, it would seem, that while for some people there have always been and always will be feasible alternatives to the family, for most people marriage and the family is the normal and virtually inevitable style of sexual relationship and parenthood.

Why then the crisis? There are a number of reasons. The community support that helps to hold a marital relationship together is not as strong as it used to be. Husbands and wives spend relatively little time together compared to what they used to in the old peasant villages. The legal and social structures of society no longer constrain a married couple to maintain appearances of unity even when all affection is gone. Finally, in the post-Freudian era we expect much more out of human intimacy than we did in years gone. by. A clean house, well-dressed children, a paycheck at the right time, good appearances in society—there was once a time when this was all one could reasonably expect from a marriage. Now we also expect self-fulfillment, personality development, a challenge, satisfaction, play. Contemporary marriages break up more often because contemporary expectations from marriage are much higher.

It is fashionable now for Christian preachers to lament the decline of the sanctity of marriage. Yet, in fact, almost all the changes mentioned above are good rather than bad from the Christian viewpoint. It is good that people have more freedom to choose; it is good to expect more warmth, satisfaction and affection from relationships; it is good to have geographical, physical and personal mobility; it is good to be dissatisfied with sham and external appearances. All of the changes that have occurred in human relationships in the past century-and-a-half are praiseworthy from the Christian viewpoint. More freedom, more emphasis on love, more stress on interpersonal intimacy is appropriate instead of a threat to a relationship which is supposed to mirror the free, open, and intimate relationship between Jesus and the church. Christians can lament the fact that human beings are not yet very skillful at responding to the challenges of the new ideals of marriage and family life, but we cannot be critical of the ideals.

And if young people are often afraid of the commitment of marriage, the reason may be that they see so much stress and strain and so little skill at generous self-giving service in the relationships between their parents. And their religions are frequently not much help. For example, it is a complete misunderstanding of this gospel passage to think that it is mainly a juridical legislation on divorce; it is, rather, an eschatological challenge. Jesus tells us that God has broken into human history and a new age of humankind has begun, that we should live lives of dedication and commitment to one another which reflect God's dedication and commitment to us. Marital intimacy is a terrible risk, because for it to be successful one must be so vulnerable that one risks the breaking of one's heart. The promise in the gospel is that even if this happens, God will be there to put the pieces back together. It is safe to take the risk.

When all we see in the gospel is an anticipation of the precise regulation of canon law, we miss the point completely.

The entire final section of Mark's gospel deals with service. This passage, then, must be understood in its context, a context of the Christian challenge to a life of service. Marital intimacy will be successful to the extent that we are ready to generously, unself-consciously, and heedlessly serve one another. For those of us who are married, the question must be how generous are we in our service of our spouse? Is it an exchange relationship, a *quid pro quo*, a matter of dealing and bartering? Or is it love heedlessly given and gratefully accepted? And those of us who are preparing for marriage should ask ourselves whether we have the courage and bravery to undertake that sort of a commitment.

41

He was setting out on a journey when a man ran up, knelt before him and put this question to him, "Good master, what must I do to inherit eternal life?" Jesus said to him, "Why do you call me good? No one is good but God alone. You know the commandments: You must not kill; You must not commit adultery; You must not steal; You must not bring false witness; You must not defraud; Honor your father and mother." *And he said to him, "Master, I have kept all these from my earliest days." Jesus looked steadily at him and loved him, and he said, "There is one thing you lack. Go and sell everything you own and give the money to the poor, and you will have treasure in heaven; then come, and follow me." But his face fell at these words and he went away sad, for he was a man of great wealth.*

Jesus looked round and said to his disciples, "How hard it is for those who have riches to enter the kingdom of God!" The disciples were astounded by these words, but Jesus insisted, "My children," he said to them "how hard it is to enter the kingdom of God! It is easier for a camel to pass through the eye of a needle than for a rich man to enter the kingdom of God." They were more astonished than ever. "In that case" they said to one another "who can be saved?" Jesus gazed at them. "For men" he said "it is impossible, but not for God: because everything is possible for God."

Peter took this up "What about us?" he asked him. "We have left everything and followed you." Jesus said, "I tell you solemnly, there is no one who has left house, brothers, sisters, father, children or land for my sake and for the sake of the gospel who will not be repaid a hundred times over, houses, brothers, sisters, mothers, children and land—not without persecutions—now in this present time and, in the world to come, eternal life."

Mark 10:17-30

HOW rich was the rich young man? Well, if he could be reborn and transplanted in American life his standard of living and his real income would have put him substantially below the $6,000 a year poverty level. The possessions of this world he had were great by the standards of his day; by the standards of your day, he would be considered one of the poorest of the poor. It is well to keep this fact in mind when we ponder the challenge of Mark's gospel. All of us are richer than the rich young man.

If we are to understand this gospel, we must first of all realize that the story of the rich young man and the story of the camel going through the eye of the needle were once two separate stories. Mark has combined them into one passage to make his point about the importance of renunciation in the life of the follower of Jesus. Neither separately nor together are the stories designed to lay down strict moral obligations, for Jesus was not a man concerned with legislating new laws. He had come into the world to challenge us. A challenge is delivered to the rich young man, and if we wish to understand the gospel, we must listen to the challenge and not worry about obligations.

The rich young man had a life plan mapped out for himself. He was obviously a serious student, a devout layman, a committed Jew, a faithful son, and a good steward of whatever were his occupational responsibilities. He could easily see, we can imagine, marriage, fatherhood, family, success, reputation, power, and prestige. It was a smooth untroubled, practical, and eminently rewarding career that stretched out ahead of him. There were no real risks, no gambles, no pitfalls; everything was neatly arranged, well planned, mapped out in advance. What he wanted from Jesus was approval and validation for such a career, and that is precisely what he did not get.

Jesus challenged the young man to a life of excitement, adventure, romance, of risk, uncertainty, and danger. The renuciation of wealth was not an end in itself, it would not make him any better a person than he already was; the critical thing for the rich young man was to break away from his own carefully drafted career scheme, to give up the security, the serenity, the peaceful complacency of his own scheme and to "go for broke" in the desperate gamble of following wherever Jesus led him. It was heady wine, indeed too heady for the rich young man. Despite his goodness, his devotion, his probity, he was not the risk-taking, adventurous, gambling type; and so he went away sad—not because the possessions as such meant all that much to him but because he was trapped in the cautious, conservative, secure life that the abundance of his possessions seemed to make possible for him. He had learned to play things safe, not to take risks; and when it was demanded of him to risk all, he was unable to respond.

The sad part of the story of the rich young man (and of the rich young man who lurks in each of us) is that, in fact, even the best charted life is not secure; even material prosperity beyond anything the rich young man could have dreamed about does not guarantee the realization of the neatly planned, carefully charted secure life. Whether we like it or not, life is an adventure, a series of risks and gambles. He who thinks he can routinize it, simplify it, make it safe, secure, and cautious, is kidding himself. He who thinks he can conservatively hoard up his life will find it slipping through his fingers. It is not a question of whether or not we gamble with our lives, for being born is a gamble; it is a question of whether we acknowledge the gamble, accept the adventure, face the inevitable risks, or whether we try to dodge, hide from, or escape the reckless romance that the lives of each of us really is.

The secret that Jesus reveals in this gospel is a powerful and important one: There is only one way to be happy and that is to believe in God's overwhelming love as it has been manifested in Jesus and, believing that love, enthusiastically follow the example of generous service that Jesus has offered. If we go to Jesus and say to him, "Master, what is the secret of life?" he says: The secret of life is that God loves you, that at the heart of the universe there is passionate love, love which makes the most powerful human love look weak by comparison." And when we say to him, "Master, how should we live?" he responds: "You should live with complete and absolute trust in God's goodness, not expecting to obtain security or protection from any of the goods of this world."

The renunciation demanded of the followers of Jesus is the renunciation of the illusion that we can be safe, cautious, conservative, complacent in our lives, that we can have well charted, neatly planned, carefully budgeted security. The renunciation demanded of the followers of Jesus is nothing more than realism; life is a risk whether we like it or not. Jesus demands that we acknowledge the risk and throw in our lot with him. He demands that we come with him as followers in what Rudyard Kipling called "the great game." For all the wild madness of a life of complete trust in Jesus and complete willingness to respond to the inspiration of the Holy Spirit, it is, in the final analysis, the safest way to live; and that is the point, not only for the rich young man but also for the rich young man in all of us.

What is demanded of the Christian, then, is not irresponsibility, not unthinking recklessness, not foolhardiness and, heaven save us, not financial stupidity. What is demanded is a life in which we hang loose and play it by ear, in which we listen very carefully to that which is best in us. And that which is best in us is the voice of the Holy Spirit. Then we quickly and resolutely seize the opportunities that come not only at the key turning points in our lives but also in little ways each day of our lives. Are we ready to go for broke with Jesus, or are we incorrigible bet hedgers? That is the question of Mark's gospel.

42

*James and John, the sons of Zebedee, approached him.
"Master," they said to him "we want you to do us a favor."
He said to them, "What is it you want me to do for you?"
They said to him, "Allow us to sit one at your right hand
and the other at your left in your glory." "You do not
know what you are asking" Jesus said to them. "Can you
drink a cup that I must drink, or be baptized with the
baptism with which I must be baptized?" They replied,
"We can." Jesus said to them, "The cup that I must drink
you shall drink, and with the baptism with which I must be
baptized you shall be baptized, but as for seats at my right
hand or my left, these are not mine to grant; they belong
to those to whom they have been allotted."*

*When the other ten heard this they began to feel indignant with James and John, so Jesus called them to him and
said to them, "You know that among the pagans their so-called rulers lord it over them, and their great men make
their authority felt. This is not to happen among you. No;
anyone who wants to become great among you must be
your servant, and anyone who wants to be first among you
must be slave to all. For the Son of Man himself did not
come to be served but to serve, and to give his life as a
ransom for many."*

Mark 10:35-45

IT is alleged that we are in a crisis of authority. The various survey organizations have shown that in the last ten
years America's confidence in its leaders in every walk of

life has declined drastically. The legislative, the executive, the judicial branches of government at all levels, business, labor, education, the churches—all have suffered drastic declines in confidence. Authority used to be able to take obedience for granted; it gave an instruction and the instruction was followed. But now the young and the not so young do not jump so readily at commands; they want to know why; they want to argue, disagree, the right to refuse, to say no. Even in the church the Pope, bishops, priests, and religious superiors no longer can command the unquestioned obedience they did in the past. Inside the family, the authority of the husband and father, the "head" of the home, seems to have been irrevocably destroyed. And the authority of parents over children apparently barely lasts beyond the middle years of grammar school. It is, indeed, a monumental crisis of authority.

There are many reasons for this crisis of authority. Usually those in authority are inclined to blame the rebelliousness, the disobedience, the cantankerousness, the contentiousness, the reckless independence of those who are supposed to obey them on the lack of proper respect evidenced by today's generations. Doubtless the rebelliousness and lack of restraint has sometimes gotten out of hand, but if we read this gospel and compare the vision of how authority ought to be exercised by those who are followers of Jesus and then look at the way it was in fact exercised, then as well as today, we are driven to the conclusion that authority is rejected because it has not often been exercised responsibly.

In his Presidential campaign, Jimmy Carter resolutely insisted that the large governmental bureaucracies must become responsible servants of the people once more. Indeed, now all candidates are saying the same things, because, like Carter, they discovered how fed up the public is with arrogant, irresponsible, self-centered, autocratic governmental bureaucracies. Although specific issues and politics are not our concern here, the point is that the widespread dissatisfaction with the authority of all large institutions in our society can ultimately be traced to the fact that the leaders in these various institutions have been exercising their authority the way Jesus says the "Gentiles" do: They have lorded it over their followers, they have thought they were great ones, they have made their importance felt. Such authority ultimately becomes illegitimate and then impotent. People reject its right to govern and then simply refuse to listen to it.

It must be honestly acknowledged that even in the church this has been something of a problem. Church leaders from parish priests on up have lorded it over the faithful, have acted like great ones, and have made their importance felt. They became so convinced of their own importance and their own power and their own sacred missions that they thought it was only required that they command and others would promptly fall into line, because, after all, didn't they act in the place of Christ? But church leaders often forgot that if indeed they were acting in the place of Christ, they ought to act the way Christ did. They ought to be willing to serve their followers even by washing their feet as Jesus did at the Last Supper; they ought to be willing to understand that the only way to achieve greatness is through service; and if they rank first, it is only as the first servant, the one who is to be most dedicated in the service of others. Some church leaders from top to bottom have forgotten this message of Jesus and they have needed to be reminded of it all through the course of human history.

But those very same Americans, who so quickly and

easily reject the "lording it over" when it happens in government, business, schools, and the church are appalled to discover that they can no longer lord it over their spouses or their children. In the past, kids did what they were told simply because their parents told them to do it. If there was ever a "lording it over" relationship, it was the parent-child relationship. And if young people have refused to accept this state of affairs, then what has come into existence is a situation in which they demand either Christian authority or no authority at all—that is to say, they demand either authority which serves and respects or they simply refuse to acknowledge the validity of that authority.

Obviously, parents must make decisions for children, particularly small ones, when they are not capable of making them themselves; but just as obviously, authoritarian, autocratic, dictatorial, arbitrary, and irrational authority no longer works with children. They reject it, they turn away from it, they escape it just as soon as they are able to. If you want to continue to influence your children's lives, if you want to continue to possess any authority over them, then you must rule them the way Jesus tells his followers to rule: "Anyone among you who aspires to greatness must serve the rest. Whoever wants to rank first among you must serve the needs of all."

In the past, those who had authority might have been able to rule by force or by appeal to the sacred nature of their offices; it won't work any more. Authority in the modern world must establish its credibility by service. Christian authority used to be an option; you could do it if you wanted to, but you didn't need it to govern. Those days seem to be over permanently; if you want to rule now, you must learn first of all how to serve. An authority of loving service turns out to be the only effective authority left in a free society. The alternative is the machinegun, the club, and the early morning visit of the Third World police state.

James and John wanted to be able to lord it over their fellow apostles, and indeed over everybody else in creation. They got the word straight from Jesus: Among his followers there simply wasn't going to be that kind of authority. It is all well and good for us to talk about our immense responsibilities and how we can only exercise those responsibilities if people are obedient to us; however, the whole point of the gospel is that people ultimately will be obedient only to those who lead them with loving service. Jesus, isn't likely to be content with any other kind of leadership from those who claim to be his brothers and sisters.

43

They reached Jericho; and as he left Jericho with his disciples and a large crowd, Bartimaeus (that is, the son of Timaeus), a blind beggar, was sitting at the side of the road. When he heard that it was Jesus of Nazareth, he began to shout and to say, "Son of David, Jesus, have pity on me." And many of them scolded him and told him to keep quiet, but he only shouted all the louder, "Son of David, have pity on me." Jesus stopped and said, "Call him here." So they called the blind man. "Courage," they said "get up; he is calling you." So throwing off his cloak, he jumped up and went to Jesus. Then Jesus spoke. "What do you want me to do for you?" "Rabbuni," the blind man said to him "Master, let me see again." Jesus said to him, "Go; your faith has saved you." And immediately his sight returned and he followed· him along the road.

Mark 10:46-52

WE are horrified when we read in the newspapers or see on television pictures of the bloody civil wars that have erupted in Ireland, Lebanon, Cyprus, and many other countries of the world. The senseless terrorist killings of innocent victims in countries like Argentina also seem to be absurd. Men and women must be blind to engage in such foolish activities, we tell ourselves. How can they ever hope to achieve peace, freedom and justice by killing one another? They seem particularly blind in such places as Ireland, Lebanon and Cyprus where the majority is not much larger than the minority and the only solution to the problems of the countries is for the two parties to learn to live with one another in peace. Moslem and Christian, Catholic and Protestant, Greek and Turk have to be blind if they don't realize that killing will only make matters worse.

But we have all seen such blindness in the people around us. We know neighbors who are so harsh and rigid and punitive with their children that it is obvious to everyone but them that they will drive the children out of the home. They, however, are blind to what they are doing to their family life. We know husbands and wives who needle each other constantly, slowly tearing apart the fabric of their marriage. Everybody else can see what is happening, but they are blind to it. And we know the man (or woman) with a very serious drinking problem. Everyone else can see what he is doing to his life, his career, his family by his drinking; but he himself is completely blind to even the existence of the problem. Perhaps we know a young person who is experimenting with drugs. We all see the dangers, but he is blind to them; he keeps telling us that he knows when to stop. Blindness, then, is not just a matter of political conflict; it's something that goes on in the lives of all of us. Everybody else can see when we are doing something self-destructive, but we are blind to it ourselves.

To make matters worse, it's easy to recognize other people's blindness, but very difficult to admit our own. We can become "past masters" at offering advice to others, at critically analyzing problems and difficulties of others, at recommending exactly the right solution for those who are blind to their own problems while it doesn't even occur to us that we ourselves may be blind—even more so than those we advise. We do not hear the ominous words of Jesus: "When the blind meet the blind, they both fall into the pit."

This gospel is about religious blindness. In the 8th, 9th, and 10th chapters of Mark's story, he is speaking directly to the religiously blind in his community, to those who so misperceive the message of Jesus as to believe that Christianity was about working miracles instead of serving other human beings, those who try to turn Jesus into a worker of marvels and miss the point of his being a representative of God's loving service. So Mark begins (8:22) and ends it with a story about blindness, warning the people who read the gospel that they had missed his point entirely. They had gotten so excited and fascinated by the marvelous, the miraculous, the wonderful, that they had forgotten the ordinary, everyday demands of generous loving service that Christianity was supposed to be all about. Bartimaeus (who may even have been known in the community to whom Mark was writing) was healed not only of physical but of spiritual blindness. So Mark warns his followers that they too must be healed of their spiritual blindness.

It is as easy for us today to be blinded by misapprehensions of Christianity as it was for the people to whom Mark wrote. We can think being a Christian means keeping certain rules—going to mass on Sunday and that sort of thing. Alternatively, we can think being a Christian means repeating the most approved political and social cliches about the "Third World." We can think Christianity simply means being an active member of our parish, or we can think it means marching on a picket line. In fact, Christianity means none of these things, although we should go to mass, and it is a good thing to be an active parishioner, and Christians should be concerned about the Third World and protest against social injustice.

For the entire 8th, 9th, and 10th chapters of his gospel, Mark has insisted over and over that Christianity is loving service of those who are around us. We must be as generous to our family, our friends, and our neighbors as God and Jesus are to us. If we do not do this, then we are as blind as those early followers of Mark who showed themselves as fascinated by miracle stories as young people are by "Star Wars." He who gives himself generously, lovingly, openly to those around him in order that their lives might be happier and better is truly a follower of Jesus of Nazareth; he really sees what Christianity is all about. Anyone else, no matter how pious, no matter how careful to keep the rules, no matter how "proper" his political and social positions, no matter how big his Sunday collection check, is not actually doing what Bartimaeus does in today's gospel—following Jesus up the road. We may think we are good Christians, we may be absolutely convinced that we are; yet blindness may be deceiving us completely, because we have forgotten what Christianity is all about.

Are we blind and leaders of the blind? One good way to tell might be to ask whether we are fed up with the emphasis on Christianity as loving service. Do we find ourselves just a bit bored by all those pictures of the suffering servant we hear? And are we just a bit offended that the church seems almost fixated on Mark's message of loving service? Has it occurred to us that the reason the church must constantly repeat the message is that most Christians most of the time throughout human history have managed to be pretty blind on the subject. They can't seem to grasp the message no matter how much the church insists on it. God has intervened in human affairs and shown himself to us through the loving service of Jesus for humankind. So it must be with us. We must dedicate ourselves to this same kind of God-revealing service to those around us. Anything else, however admirable it may be, is not Christian.

44

Seeing the crowds, he went up the hill. There he sat down and was joined by his disciples. Then he began to speak. This is what we taught them:

> *"How happy are the poor in spirit;*
> *theirs is the kingdom of heaven.*
> *Happy the gentle:*
> *they shall have the earth for their heritage.*
> *Happy those who mourn:*
> *they shall be comforted.*
> *Happy those who hunger and thirst for what is right:*
> *they shall be satisfied.*
> *Happy the merciful:*
> *they shall have mercy shown them.*
> *Happy the pure in heart:*
> *they shall see God.*
> *Happy the peacemakers:*
> *they shall be called sons of God.*
> *Happy those who are persecuted in the cause of right:*
> *theirs is the kingdom of heaven.*

"Happy are you when people abuse you and persecute you and speak all kinds of calumny against you on my account. Rejoice and be glad, for your reward will be great in heaven; this is how they persecuted the prophets before you."

Matthew 5:1-12

AMERICAN Catholics were quite rightly proud of the canonization of St. Elizabeth Seton. She was the first native-born American to become a saint; and while saints don't seem to occupy our thinking as much as they used to and canonizations get much less attention than they once did, it is still nice to know that "one of our own" has made it. Of course, St. Elizabeth is very different from most of us in many respects. She was a convert; most of us are born Catholics. She was an aristocrat, and most of us are either working or middle class. Unlike most religious, she was a married woman and a mother. For aristocratic widows who become converts and sisters, Elizabeth Seton is an ideal model; for the rest of us, she remains an important model in one decisive respect: Saints are happy people, no matter what happens. What really counts about St. Elizabeth Seton is not her nationality or her background or her state in life or her accomplishment as the founder of the Daughters of Charity. What counts is that she was an example of happiness.

Life is often a very grim and morose business. We lose our youthful enthusiasms and energies long before we are thirty. Disillusionment, cynicism, frustration seem to spoil our lives, blight our dreams, shake off our hopes. We may be able to settle down to a relatively peaceful and trouble-free existence; but it often seems to us that we have settled for so much less than we once thought we would be able to get. Our physical energies run down; we don't bounce back as quickly as we used to. We don't wake up in the morning with the ambition and drive we once had. Time both goes more quickly and seems to hang more heavily on-our hands. We are caught in monotonies, routines, ruts we cannot climb out of. Life's pleasures lack the savor they used to have. Winter colds and summer flu come earlier and last longer, leaving us more exhausted. Life is not all bad, but it certainly isn't a bowl of cherries either. We find ourselves wondering whether there are any surprises left in the world, whether any really good things will ever happen again.

And then something does happen. A little child toddles awkwardly across the room and looks up at us with bright eyes and a wide, friendly grin. The kid is happy—shallowly, superficially, naively happy. He will doubtless grow up to become as weary and worn as we are, but in that moment we get a glimpse, a faint hint, in the child's smile that there might be more to life than our weary cynicism. The child, for all his inexperience and naivety, may know something we don't through his youthful enthusiastic wonder.

A clear, crisp autumn day begins after what seems like weeks of gray rain and drizzle. The sky is blue, the air is clean, the colors of autumn are all around us. Again, for a brief, quick interlude, before we become lost in our daily routine, we sense that the blue sky may tell us more than the gray one; the clean, clear air reveals more than the drizzle, and the joy of the autumn radiance is something more fundamental than our own grim, morose daily routine. Maybe, just maybe, there is something else at work in the universe, something that is trying desperately to break through to us in the smile of a child and in the bright clarity of an autumn day.

Saints like Elizabeth Seton are simply people who take the smile of a child and the wonder of an autumn morning seriously. They believe in a vision of life that is revealed in such passing interludes; they believe in the possibility of wonder, in the reality of joy, in the ecstasy of simply being alive. They are just as likely to grow weary as we are, just as prone to sickness, just as open to discouragement, just as keenly aware of the pain of frustration, disillusionment and failure. But what makes the saints different from us is that they do not permit their lives to acquire the gray, grim color of discouragement, frustration, routine and failure. They shake off boredom, disillusionment, weariness, and live lives that are not gray-tinged but lives that radiate the deep rich colors of autumn or the bright, shining eyes of a little child. We ordinary people wonder why life is so heavy and monotonous; the saints wonder why there is so much brilliance and joy in the world.

It is a mistake to think that the saints are fundamentally different from us in some kind of physical or chemical way. Some of them have certain special advantages. St. Elizabeth Seton had a superb education, powerful friends, immense personal self-confidence. But not all the saints had such advantages by any means. The more spectacular saints, the ones that get all the public notice, also seem to have had special gifts of divine grace; but the ordinary saints—whose feast we celebrate today—had no extraordinary talents and no extraordinary graces. They were and are fundamentally no different from us in biology, physiology, chemistry, psychology. They kept joy and wonder alive through the frustrations and disappointments of life, and it was no easier for them than it is for us. They woke up in the morning with "the blahs" every bit as often as we do. To keep their wonder and their joy alive despite the blahs of life they had to put in an immense amount of effort. They suffered many, many failures. The secret to being one of all the saints is not to exorcise the blahs from life; it is rather never to cease fighting against them.

When you encounter a saint, or at least someone who is obviously a very good Christian, the experience is much like that of a glorious autumn morning or the bright, shiny face of a happy child. It is revelatory; it reveals to us what life is all about. So it should be with our own lives. When those who are not followers of Jesus of Nazareth encounter us, they should see the joy, the hope and the surprise of the resurrection in our personality. On the Feast of All the Saints, we should ask ourselves how many of those who know us well would consider our personality to be a revelation? How many would consider an encounter with us to be like an autumn morning or a smiling child? Why have we lost our joy? Where has our capacity to wonder gone?

45

*He entered Jericho and was going through the town when a
man whose name was Zacchaeus made his appearance; he
was one of the senior tax collectors and a wealthy man. He
was anxious to see what kind of man Jesus was, but he was
too short and could not see him for the crowd; so he ran
ahead and climbed a sycamore tree to catch a glimpse of
Jesus who was to pass that way. When Jesus reached the
spot he looked up and spoke to him: "Zacchaeus, come
down. Hurry, because I must stay at your house today."
And he hurried down and welcomed him joyfully. They
all complained when they saw what was happening. "He
has gone to stay at a sinner's house" they said. But Zacchaeus stood his ground and said to the Lord, "Look, sir,
I am going to give half my property to the poor, and if I
have cheated anybody I will pay him back four times the
amount." And Jesus said to him, "Today salvation has
come to this house, because this man too is a son of Abraham; for the Son of Man has come to seek out and save
what was lost."*

Luke 19:1-10

IT is not so easy to make visits to the Blessed Sacrament
as it used to be. Fear of vandalism and violent crime has
forced many parishes to lock their churches at times when
mass is not being said. We can no longer drop into church
on the way home from school in the afternoon or on a
walk in the early evening (who walks in the evening these
days?) or on the way to the store in the morning. The old

198

Catholic practice of visits to the Blessed Sacrament seems to be a casualty—at least in the cities—not so much of the Vatican Council renewal and reform but of the increased dangers of urban life. Still, there are a few churches into which one can duck briefly for a few moments of peaceful respite from the hustle and turbulence of life. When we get an opportunity to make such a visit, we find ourselves recalling many such peaceful interludes from the past and wishing that there were more of them in our life today.

It may only be our childhood training, but more likely it is something deeper in our personality that when we cross the threshold of a church we feel we are leaving the outside world behind and coming into a place that belongs to God. The church is God's place—the whole world is God's place, of course, when we stop to think about it—in a special way because this is the place that is completely dedicated to him. Sometimes we have to use our churches for other things, for meeting halls, classrooms, lecture halls. It may be that this is a bit disconcerting to many of us, for even though there are good reasons and just cause, still it seems to be just a little bit profane to use the church as anything else but God's special place. However, it is curiously true that when the church becomes a church once again, it takes on the atmosphere of being God's place regardless of what other things may have transpired in it.

So when we come into the church from outside, at least ideally, we cross a great divide and pass through a massive gate, enter through thick, heavy veils, and the noises, the worries, distractions, fears, demands, responsibilities, expectations, longing, disappointments of our daily life slip away from us and we come into God's presence. In church we feel that we are before God in the same way that Zacchaeus was present before Jesus, first from his treetop lookout and then when Jesus came to be a guest in his house. The church is a place where God comes to be a guest in our world in a special way.

Christianity is not absolutely required to have a sacred place. It is a religion of a God who is everywhere, who can be worshiped everywthere. Indeed, Jesus was quite critical of those who made the sacred place so much the center of their religion that nothing else seemed important —and he would be critical of us if we became so obsessed with church buildings as to forget that there are other and more important aspects to Christianity. But still the early Christians, open as they were to all good things in the human condition, recognized the importance of the human need to have a sacred place, and transformed the old temple buildings and law courts into Christian dwellings into which God came to visit them as Jesus came to visit Zacchaeus.

So the sacred place comes to represent the human conviction that God, whoever and whatever he might be, does come to visit his creatures. In some fashion or other God is present to us; the sacred place represents our hope that he is present to us in such a way that we can do reverence to him, speak to him, ask him for favors, thank him for his blessings. The Christian church is a special kind of sacred place because it represents the Christian conviction that God is present to us not as an overlord, not as a master, not as a solemn judge, not as a grand executioner but as a friend who, like Jesus, would come to have dinner with a feisty, pushy but loveable little fellow like Zacchaeus. The church, be it the great St. John Lateran, the cathedral church of all the world, or the smallest and simplest parish church, is a place where God comes to sup with us.

But the Christian also believes that it is possible for one

place to be sacred because every place is sacred. God may be in a church in a special way, but that is a concession to our human religious needs. In fact, God has come as a friend who will have supper with us not only in a church but in the whole world in which we live. The entire world is the banquet place where we sup at the table of the Lord. We go into church to escape the unrest, the distractions, the noise and bother of everyday life, we come into church to sup with the Lord God who is our friend; but then we go forth from the church with the message of bringing the peace and joy of that friendship out into the harried, restless, anxious world from which we have come. The church is not a place of escape so much as it is a place of transformation, and we come into the church every Sunday (or every Saturday afternoon) not so much to get away from it all, not so much to find a little bit of peace and quiet, but rather to be transformed, to store up the joy, enthusiasm, and spiritual energy to enable us to go out and transform the world around us. Zacchaeus publicly transformed his whole life while Jesus was visiting at his house, and ever after was a very different sort of man(though one suspects he remained energetic and feisty). So when we come forth from visiting with God in the house where he sups with us, we too should leave transformed. From the Christian point of view, that's the only reason for having a church.

Do we go to church to find a place of refuge, to hide from the challenges of the world? Or do we find in church the joy of a visit with the Lord, coming out renewed and confirmed in our faith and invigorated by his peaceful presence? And do we look to find him in the world too? The church may be where God is in a special way, but he is everywhere; the world is God's place, and he lives in it and in each of us.

46

Jesus said to them, "Is not the reason why you go wrong,
that you understand neither the scriptures nor the power
of God? For when they rise from the dead, men and
women do not marry; no, they are like the angels in heaven.
Now about the dead rising again, have you never read in
the Book of Moses, in the passage about the Bush, how
God spoke to him and said: I am the God of Abraham,
the God of Isaac and the God of Jacob? *He is God, not*
of the dead, but of the living. You are very much mis-
taken."

One of the scribes who had listened to them debating
and had observed how well Jesus had answered them, now
came up and put a question to him, "Which is the first of
all the commandments?" Jesus replied, "This is the first:
Listen, Israel, the Lord our God is the one Lord, and you
must love the Lord your God with all your heart, with all
your soul, with all your mind and with all your strength.
The second is this: You must love your neighbor as yourself. *There is no commandment greater than these." The*
scribe said to him, "Well spoken, Master; what you have
said is true: that he is one and there is no other."

Mark 12:24-32

THE days grow shorter; the leaves fall from the trees.
Thanksgiving draws near, and once again we begin to
hear the strange, frightening imagery of the "end-of-the-
year" gospels. The sun will darken, the moon will not shed
its light, the stars will fall out of the skies, the Son of Man

will come out of the clouds with power and glory. Many of us remember the first time we heard these gospels as grade school children sitting in our parish churches. The story sounded scary then and, while it is not so scary now, it is still baffling. Heaven and earth will pass away, but when, how and why?

In these end-of-the-year gospels we hear language that is totally unfamiliar to us. It comes from a different "language games," a different style of thought, a different mode of thinking. Indeed, so great is the difference that we not only have a hard time making sense out of language, we also have a hard time trying to figure out what it meant to the people who did use it. It is wild, passionate, poetic imagery that fills these end-of-the-year gospels, and that's fair enough. The images are different from those we use, and that's fair enough, too. But to make matters worse, they are different even from any image we could think of using.

Yet, this end-of-the-world rhetoric, with its darkened sun and lightless moon and stars falling from the skies, was as much a part of the matrix of the thought at the time of Jesus as evolution or social class are parts of the matrix of thought during our own time. Apocalyptic language was language everybody used and everybody took for granted not only in Jewish culture but in many of the surrounding pagan cultures as well. What distinguishes the apocalyptic imagery of the gospel is that by comparison with other religious expressions of the day, the gospel imagery of the end of the world was mild and restrained; and it would appear that Jesus himself was even more restrained in his use of such language. Much of what we have in the end-of-the-year gospels is in fact religious or theological reflection in apocalyptic imagery on the much more restrained original teachings of Jesus.

We find ourselves wondering whether the people who seemed so familiar, so at home, with such wild, destructive word pictures literally expected the sun and the moon to be blacked out and the stars to fall from the sky. Did they actually expect that the world was coming to an end? What makes this question hard to answer is that it is not a question that would have occurred to them at all. As best one can judge, if they were asked it, they would have said that no, they did not necessarily expect the stars to fall from the sky but yes, they did expect a dramatic intervention of God which would lead to the end of the old age and the beginning of the new. One must remember that the old Greek empires had faded and the new Roman empire had come into being, completely reordering the map of the Mediterranean world. There was a very powerful consciousness that decisive changes were at work; there had been changes for four hundred and fifty years before Jesus, and would be for seventy or eighty years after him. Quite correctly, as it turned out, the people of the time knew there was a turning point.

Jesus came to announce a new age of the earth, the beginning of the new humanity, the recreation of the human race. It was inevitable that the religious language of the time would be used to convey this notion, which seemed so fundamentally similar to and parallel with popular expectations of signs and wonders from the skies. But Jesus' revelation would not come that way; it would come from a new perception of the relationship between God and humankind. God was involved in the human condition in a deep, intimate, and powerfully loving way. It was the work of the love of God revealed in Jesus that would transform the world. The dramatic events would not be stars falling from the skies or the dead gathered from the four winds; the really dramatic events would be the manifestation, and then the operation in the human condition, of the overwhelmingly powerful love of God. That is the decisive event which the wild rhetoric of the end-of-the-year gospels is attempting to describe.

All this is a rather lengthy explanation; but there is no escaping it if we want to break through the surface imagery of these end-of-the-year gospels, to transcend the limitations of the culture that produced the imagery and to understand the basic message contained there—a message as critically important today as it was long ago. If Jesus had come today, he certainly would have chosen a different way of saying it, but the message today would be the same: God is near to us with his love. That love presents us with, indeed demands of us, a decisive choice; and that choice is the great event of our life—to accept and respond to the love that God has offered or to turn away from it in fear, skepticism and distrust. In effect, the message of Jesus in the end-of-the-year gospels is that the end of the world is not some unspecified day of wrath in the future but a highly specified day of decision now. The end of the world is *today,* because the opportunity of responding to God is *today.*

But will there be a last judgment? Will there be an end of the world? Will Jesus actually return personally to wrap up what he began? Again, we must distinguish carefully between the language in which the message is conveyed and the message itself. The core of the message is not a great assembly of people in the valley of Armageddon and a judge riding in on clouds to pronounce sentence. The core of the message is that what Jesus began will eventually be brought to fulfillment; the power of God's love will eventually complete the work that Jesus began. Details of how that will be accomplished are beyond our knowledge, but they are relatively unimportant; God's love as revealed in Jesus will eventually triumph over evil and sin.

47

So Pilate went back into the Praetorium and called Jesus
to him, "Are you the king of the Jews?" he asked. Jesus
replied, "Do you ask this of your own accord, or have
others spoken to you about me?" Pilate answered, "Am
I a Jew? It is your own people and the chief priests who
have handed you over to me: what have you done?" Jesus
replied, "Mine is not a kingdom of this world; if my king-
dom were of this world, my men would have fought to
prevent my being surrendered to the Jews. But my king-
dom is not of this kind." "So you are a king then?" said
Pilate. "It is you who say it" answered Jesus. "Yes, I am
a king. I was born for this, I came into the world for this:
to bear witness to the truth; and all who are on the side
of truth listen to my voice."

John 18:33-37

IT would appear that at least for the time being there are
no new attempts to create the "Jesus for our time." We
have seen in recent years Jesus as a gun-toting revolutionary, as the befuddled rock hero of *Superstar,* as Jesus, the
flower-child of *Godspell.* We have also suffered through
the tormented Jesus of the novelist Nikos Kazantzakis and
have heard of the pornographic Jesus of the Danish film-
makers and the surrealistic Jesus of *The Passover Plot.*
There now seems to be a breather; but we can be sure that
before very long a new portrait of Jesus will come down
the turnpike, purporting to offer at last the real truth about
"the man nobody knows."

The figure and personage of Jesus is endlessly fascinating. Painters must draw him, sculptors carve him out of stone, novelists write stories about him; and he seems to have been played recently by a whole host of motion picture actors (not yet including Frank Sinatra). It is difficult to escape the charm, the power, the magnetism of Jesus. But it is also very, very difficult to capture him. Those who claim they have presented to us the definitive Jesus in fact have usually taken one aspect of his personality and emphasized it to the exclusion of all the rest. They usually succeed only in producing an idol—a Jesus that is identified with their cause, who, in the process of identification, ceases to be Jesus at all. The Jesus who is reduced to a formula (usually that of those who have created him) and is not an enigma, a mystery, a challenge, a sign of contradiction isn't the real Jesus at all.

The charge against Jesus by his enemies was that he was a political messiah—a phony and trumped up charge made despite the fact that repeatedly through his life he had denied and refused such political leadership. His friends had tried to make him a messiah; he turned them down. Now his enemies put him on trial for being the very thing he refused to be. Pilate asks him about the charge and he makes it very clear that whatever leadership he may have has nothing to do with political kingdoms. Still he was executed as a political revolutionary. Through the course of history his enthusiastic followers would attempt to identify him with political causes—be they causes of the status quo or the revolution. The guerrilla Jesus with a gun on his shoulder or the Jesus who underwrites and sustains American capitalism is the Jesus of the mobs in Galilee and the Jesus of the charges of the Sanherdrin; but it is not the real Jesus at all.

The mistake of the political revolutionaries of Galilee

and of the 1960s—and also the mistake of those who executed Jesus—was to try to capture him in something less than a paradox or a seeming contradiction. Of course there were tremendously powerful political implications of the message of love and justice that Jesus brought, implications for human freedom, human dignity, and human growth that would eventually transform the world. But Jesus could not be simply identified with or reduced to any particular social policy, program, or plan. The passion for love and justice that animated him was too big for any simple formula; to try to reduce it to one is to try to relativize the absolute, to make the infinite finite, and to freeze at a given point in time and space something that speaks to all men at all times. Christians must do their best when they follow the message of Jesus to develop political programs and plans of their own; but they are guilty of idolatry when they identify those plans with Jesus.

Similarly, the counterculture Jesus of *Superstar* and *Godspell* was not untrue, just terribly incomplete. There *was* in the message of Jesus a judgment of all up-tight, hypocritical, rigid, insensitive, unsympathetic individuals and societies; Jesus *was* an outcast, someone who simply did not fit in the "establishment" of his time. But neither did he fit into the counterculture of his time. The Zealot revolutionaries of his time and the Essene dropouts in the desert liked him even less than did the scribes and Pharisees and Sadducees. If Jesus was "antiestablishment," he was also anticounterculture; for he preached commitment to other human beings and to human society rather than withdrawal from them. He preached highly disciplined responsibility for the loving service of others rather than a spontaneous "do your own thing" approach to human life. Jesus is the king we honor today because he is too big, too mysterious, too powerful, too overwhelming in the love of God which he reveals to fit into anybody's formula, anybody's program, anybody's simple image, anybody's faith in a comfortable, cozy Jesus who reinforces the prejudices, rigidity, narrowness and insensitivity of one's own perspective. A Jesus who is not a challenge to us (as well as to others) is not a real Jesus at all.

Jesus, then, is not a satisfying answer; he is a troubling question. When he satisfies us, reassures us, makes us complacent, reinforces our own natural propensities, then he isn't Jesus at all. When he shakes us up, startles us, stirs us out of our complacency, demands that we change, rethink, re-examine, re-evaluate, refocus, he is the real Jesus, the Jesus who came to be a sign of contradiction, who came to cast fire on the earth, who came to stir us up with the shattering, mysterious, overwhelming news of God's love for us. Jesus is the king we honor at the end of the church year precisely because he is a challenging question rather than a reassuring answer. And the question is, "Are you ready to respond to the invitation to the wedding banquet organized by my Father in heaven?"

Who is the Jesus that reassures each one of us and makes us complacent? What is the image of Jesus that most effectively reinforces our own self-satisfaction, our own prejudices, our own narrowness, our own passion to have things nice and easy, simple and orderly? Who is our equivalent of the *Superstar* Jesus or the guerrilla Jesus? Who is the Jesus that makes us the good guys and other people the bad guys? Who is *that* Jesus? Well, whichever one he is— and he is different for each one of us—is not the real Jesus at all. We should forget about that Jesus and pay close attention to the one who shakes us up, disturbs us, and makes us wonder who we are and where we are really going.

48

"Be on your guard, stay awake, because you never know when the time will come. It is like a man traveling abroad: he has gone from home, and left his servants in charge, each with his own task; and he has told the doorkeeper to stay awake. So stay awake, because you do not know when the master of the house is coming, evening, midnight, cockcrow, dawn; if he comes unexpectedly, he must not find you asleep. And what I say to you I say to all: Stay awake!"

Mark 13:33-37

SO much of our lives is spent waiting. When we were children we waited until it was time to go to school, then we waited for our grammar school, high school and college graduations. We wait until we get married, we wait for our first job, we wait for the coming of our children, we wait to get old, we wait to die. We wait for good news, we wait for bad news; we wait for spring to come, we wait for the weekend. Perhaps, like the two characters in the play, we wait for Godot, who never comes. Rarely does it turn out that the things we wait for are nearly as good in the event as they are in the expectation.

Our lives are filled with loneliness. There is the deep and the intense loneliness which comes when someone we love is absent. There is the sharp loneliness of homesickness; the dull ache when we miss family and friends through a long separation, the poignant loneliness of the last few weeks, the last few days, the last few hours before we are

In Loving Memory of

Bernard T. Murray

WHO DIED

DECEMBER 5, 1977

THE LORD BE WITH YOU,
and

May the angels lead you into Paradise, may the Martyrs receive you at your coming, and take you to Jerusalem, the holy city. May the choirs of the Angels receive you, and may you with the once poor Lazarus, have rest everlasting. Amen.

May the Souls of all the faithful departed, through the mercy of God, rest in peace. Amen.

Chapel of the Acres

ETERNA – Series

rough all our loneliness o return, we wait to go in us, we wait for our loneliness go hand in sses rapidly; but when ime hangs heavy and rminable. We look at and then look at the

eliness which is more tice it. When we do es us. This loneliness times of joy, not in lfillment, not in times is the loneliness that rything we want and loneliness of a meal her the loneliness that comes at the end of a pleasant and delicious dinner with our family and friends. We seem to have everything we could possibly ask for and still something is missing.

It is in these moments that we recognize an acute loneliness that has been with us all the time but which we simply haven't noticed before. The moment quickly passes away and we forget that sharp stab of loneliness that interrupts a delightful occasion; but it will return again and again in our lives. Something is missing—or is it Someone? Who is it? Where is he? Why do we want him? When will he return?

When we are separated from those we love, we can easily explain the anguish of our life as the result of that separation; but when we are united with them and there is still anguish, we are forced to face the dismaying fact that as human creatures we are simply never satisfied. Give any other animal food, warmth, shelter, companionship and it will seek for nothing else; there is no restlessness, no unease, no anxiety, no waiting for some mysteriously absent other. The nonhuman animal is satisfied when basic needs are met; the human animal continues to wait, to expect, to seek for the Something or Someone to which we cannot even give a name.

Occasionally when we are caught in these interludes of baffling loneliness we get a hint of just who it is we are expecting. It is Someone "out there" who can satisfy all our longings and who cares for us the way a warm and gentle mother does for an amusing, charming and occasionally naughty child. There is out there, we sense in these brief moments of insight, a love so powerful, so strong, so passionate, so overwhelming that we realize we cannot even begin to plumb its depths. And that is the one we are expecting; it is him for whom we wait.

Advent is a time when the church tries to stir this sense of expectation and waiting out of the depths of our personalities and make us face it, instead of ducking away from its challenge as we normally do. For it is during Advent season, when the days grow short and skies grow dark, that the abiding loneliness of human life is hardest to escape. And as we prepare for Christmas, the church tells us who it is for whom we are waiting and why our lives are lonely without him.

49

In due course John the Baptist appeared; he preached in the wilderness of Judaea and this was his message: "Repent, for the kingdom of heaven is close at hand." This was the man the prophet Isaiah spoke of when he said:

A voice cries in the wilderness:
Prepare a way for the Lord,
make his paths straight.

This man John wore a garment made of camel-hair with a leather belt round his waist, and his food was locusts and wild honey. Then Jerusalem and all Judaea and the whole Jordan district made their way to him, and as they were baptized by him in the river Jordan they confessed their sins. But when he saw a number of Pharisees and Saducees coming for baptism he said to them, "Brood of vipers, who warned you to fly from the retribution that is coming? But if you are repentant, produce the appropriate fruit, and do not presume to tell yourselves, 'We have Abraham for our father,' because, I tell you, God can raise children for Abraham from these stones. Even now the ax is laid to the roots of the trees, so that any tree which fails to produce good fruit will be cut down and thrown on the fire. I baptize you in water for repentance, but the one who follows me is more powerful than I am, and I am not fit to carry his sandals; he will baptize you with the Holy Spirit and fire. His winnowing-fan is in his hand; he will clear his threshing-floor and gather his wheat into the barn; but the chaff he will burn in a fire that will never go out."

Matthew 3:1-12

THERE were hints in the papers some time ago that the long-awaited "cure" for the common cold might be just around the corner. Medical science has apparently made a major breakthrough in dealing with virus infections. Maybe the next virus we will be able to dispose of will be that of the cold. No one will miss the common cold. We will tell our children and grandchildren about it while they listen in disbelief that there ever could have been an ailment so annoying and so tenacious. We will forget it and they will never know how splendid it was to wake up one morning to discover the cold was gone. No more cough, no more sneeze, no more runny nose. It was almost like being born again; you couldn't believe how fortunate you were and rejoiced all day long that your miserable cold was at last over.

This gospel story is like a light flashing on in a room, a sudden jolt of electric current when we unguardedly touch a socket, a burst of health and energy after a long sickness. We have a sense that things are moving as we hear the gospel story, that there is action, that we are well into the first act of the drama, and the leading character is about to make his or her entrance on stage. The past is over and done with; no more darkness, misery, fear; the future is about to begin. We know this, of course, because we've heard the story of John the Baptist around Christmastime for as long as we can remember Christmas. The weather grows cool, the days shorten, but the pace of life speeds up. Christmas is at hand.

We are so used to hearing the John the Baptist story before Christmas that we almost don't notice that he came long after Christmastime. The gospel account really deals with a time long after the birth of Jesus. The gospel, in fact, is a preparation not so much for Christmas as for the public life of Jesus. John the Baptist was indeed the herald, but not so much the herald of Christmastime as the herald of the final and fulfilling act of the drama of Jesus. Why does the church bring John the Baptist to us at this time of year?

The answer is that the church insists on seeing the coming of Jesus, his advent into the world, as one continuous action and not as a series of discrete and disparate events. Good Friday and Easter are present in Christmas just as Christmas is present in Good Friday and Easter; for they are all acts by which God's great love is revealed to us and through which we are called to respond to that great love by offering our gracious love to other human beings. Christmas reveals God's love; so does Easter; so does Good Friday. The joy of Christmas contains within it the sorrow of Good Friday and the triumph of Easter. All are linked together because they are all part of one stupendous act of self-disclosure by God. The church can easily put the John the Baptist story in this time before Christmas because Christmas is not merely the birth of Jesus; it is the beginning of the total revelation of Jesus and contains within it, in preliminary form, the whole story of God's great love for us.

The human race, in other words, was coming to the end of a long period of low-grade infection, fear, distrust, hatred. The infection had not killed off the human race, but it kept us sick, weary, tired, despondent. And then Jesus came, the sprout from the root of Jesse described in the beautiful, poetic word-paintings of the first reading— justice a band around his waist, faithfulness a belt on his hips, possessing the spirit of wisdom and understanding, bringing together the wolf and the lamb, the leopard and the kid, the cow and the bear. It was a monumental, dramatic, overwhelming revolution which turned everything upside down. And turned upside down, the world suddenly

215

seemed to make sense, as G. K. Chesterton once said. Sickness was over; the road back to health lay before us. The trumpet call of John the Baptist is like the first morning we awake confident that, at long last, the infection that has weakened has begun to go away.

"But," we say, "all you have to do is look at this morning's newspaper to see that hatred, suspicion, distrust, injustice, oppression still dominate the world. What difference does the coming of Jesus make, what difference does the celebration of Christmas make? Isn't humankind as sick as it ever was?" The only answer is that the journey toward full health is a long and painful one. The human race is beginning to recover from its illness of sin, but it still has a long way to go. The cure depends ultimately on the response of each one of us. As long as there is hatred and fear in our hearts, then we stand as barriers to the health that Jesus wants to communicate to all of us. We are the last lingering microbes that keep humanity sick. So we ask ourselves, when we hear John the Baptist talk about the winnowing fan that clears the threshing floor, Do our lives, when reviewed this Advent, look like lives of wheat or chaff? Do we get gathered into the barn, or do we get set on fire?

50

Now John in his prison had heard what Christ was doing and he sent his disciples to ask him, "Are you the one who is to come, or have we got to wait for someone else?" Jesus answered, "Go back and tell John what you hear and see; the blind see again, and the lame walk, lepers are cleansed, and the deaf hear, and the dead are raised to life and the Good News is proclaimed to the poor; and happy is the man who does not lose faith in me."

As the messengers were leaving, Jesus began to talk to the people about John: "What did you go out into the wilderness to see? A reed swaying in the breeze? No? Then what did you go out to see? A man wearing fine clothes? Oh no, those who wear fine clothes are to be found in palaces. Then what did you go out for? To see a prophet? Yes, I tell you, and much more than a prophet: he is the one of whom scripture says:

Look, I am going to send my messenger before you;
he will prepare your way before you.

"I tell you solemnly, of all the children born of women, a greater than John the Baptist has never been seen; yet the least in the kingdom of heaven is greater than he is."

Matthew 11:2-11

NOTE very carefully what Jesus says to the followers of John the Baptist in the gospel story. They come to inquire whether Jesus is the expected one, the messiah for whom generations have longed and hoped, the man who would begin those dramatic events which that rough, fiery leader knew in his soul were about to happen. Jesus first of all refers to that passage in Isaiah which we hear in today's first reading, with which all Jews were very familiar. Then he points out that precisely those surprising things which Isaiah had described seemed to be happening in his ministry. In effect, he says to the followers of John, "What do you think? Isaiah said there would be surprises as dramatic as the desert blooming and the parched land producing crops. If all these wonderful events are occurring, then don't you think this might indeed be the beginning of a new age on earth?"

Jesus was appealing to the wonder and the surprise of his ministry as proof that he indeed did represent that which all Israelites and indeed all humankind in some way had been longing for—a fresh, new beginning. It was precisely the surprise component of his mission that Jesus thought should be of decisive importance for those who wondered about it. Note that the biggest surprise of all is one not mentioned by Isaiah—the ordinary folk, the poor people, the despised common man, the Jewish equivalent of "Middle America" or "the silent majority" was having the Good News preached to them. Jesus says to his questioners, in effect, "Sure, there have been miracles, and those are surprises, but isn't it even more surprising that I am preaching to the ordinary folk—not just the rich, the powerful, the ecclesiastical dignitaries, and the pious. And the ordinary folk are listening to me."

Jesus was a wonder-worker, indeed, but the wonderful things he did were not proof so much as occasions for surprise. Jesus was not trying to beat people over the head with his miraculous powers so they would believe in him;

rather the wonderful things of his ministry—especially the wonder of preaching the gospel to ordinary folk—were meant to shake up, disconcert, shatter, challenge, excite, awaken, to call forth out of ordinary routine monotony, to make people think. They said the messiah would make you wonder; Jesus said to the followers of the Baptist, "Here I am making you wonder. What more proof do you need?"

It could easily be said that the principal goal of the mission of Jesus then, and the principal purpose of his life and work for us even today is to stir us up, make us wonder, to shatter us with surprise, to disconcert us out of the ordinary and the routine. A Jesus who does not surprise us, does not baffle us, does not disconcert us, who does not make us wonder, is no Jesus at all. A miracle-worker come to establish proof that turns faith into a matter of mathematical certainty is not the real Jesus. A Jesus who associates with the poor, the oppressed, the sinner, the politically unfashionable (like the publicans), a Jesus who stubbornly refuses to fit into anyone's category or even to give clear and simple answers to anyone's questions (note that he leaves the Baptist's followers to answer their own questions) is the Jesus who preached at Galilee and the Jesus whom we are all committed to follow.

Christmas is a great surprise—the children wide-eyed at the sight of the tree and its stack of gifts merely hint at the surprise we all feel during this time of the year. Indeed, things are all wrong in our lives if it is only the children who are surprised. The older we get, the more experience we've had, the more surprises that we have had in our lives should make us realize that the greatest surprise of all is the grace of God, the grace of a wonder that we did not expect, of a shattering event to disconcert us, to catch us off balance, a love we didn't deserve, a kindness beyond our expectations, a response more enthusiastic than we dared hope for, a joy exceeding all dreams. To ignore these surprises, these graces, to refuse to see them, is the worst sort of spiritual blindness.

Just as there is surprise at Christmas-time, so there is a bit of grace in every surprise we have ever experienced. If we want to know what Jesus was like and what life is about and what the fulfillment of human life will lead to, then we ought to reflect on the events of wonder and surprise that have graced our life and have given us moments of greatest joy. If there is still a capacity for surprise, if there is still wide-eyed wonder left in our existence, then we are followers of Jesus of Nazareth, and we do not have to go away like the disciples of John, trying to figure out what he was talking about. But if there is no wonder, no excitement, no surprises left in our existence, then something is terribly wrong with us, and this Advent season is a time we desperately need to set our lives in order.

When was the last time we were surprised? Did we really wonder over it? Did it really excite us? Did it really cheer us up? Did we feel good about it, or was it but a ripple on the smooth lake of boredom that is our daily existence? Can we remember a surprise? If we can't, what has happened to us?

51

This is how Jesus Christ came to be born. His mother Mary was betrothed to Joseph; but before they came to live together she was found to be with child through the Holy Spirit. Her husband Joseph, being a man of honor and wanting to spare her publicity, decided to divorce her informally. He had made up his mind to do this when the angel of the Lord appeared to him in a dream and said, "Joseph son of David, do not be afraid to take Mary home as your wife, because she has conceived what is in her by the Holy Spirit. She will give birth to a son and you must name him Jesus, because he is the one who is to save his people from their sins." Now all this took place to fulfill the words spoken by the Lord through the prophet:

> The virgin will conceive and give birth to a son
> and they will call him Emmanuel,

a name which means "God-is-with-us." When Joseph woke up he did what the angel of the Lord had told him to do: he took his wife to his home.

Matthew 1:18-24

OUR early ancestors were very frightened by winter. It was not merely that it was cold and that the animals and plants which provided their food were no longer around, it was not merely that the supplies stored up for the winter were depleted too rapidly; it was also that the night grew longer and the day shorter. As time went on, human-kind

221

grew skilled at charting the movements of the heavens, and they were able to predict that on one morning in the middle of winter, the sun rose at an ever so slightly higher place on the horizon; that meant the day would be longer than the day before. The worst was over; light would conquer darkness once again. The sun had returned; the sign was in the heavens; life began again.

The story we read in this gospel is a simple, gentle, lovely story. God had fallen in love with Mary, and he chose her to bring Jesus into the world. There were many similar stories of divine incarnations in ancient times. Some of them were bizarre and some grotesque. This was completely different in kind and quality. The God who was going to come into the world through Mary seemed to be a quiet, discreet, almost self-effacing God, who sent his angel to politely inquire whether the young woman wanted to cooperate. She quietly and confidently agreed, and her baffled husband was also politely informed about the event. A strange sort of God this must be who deals so gently, so discreetly, so thoughtfully, so courteously. No loud explosions, no fireworks, no dramatic announcements—it all happened so quietly, so gently, so subtly that scarcely anyone else noticed. As a sign it didn't look like much at all. It has taken on sign value only for those who are able to see what it means.

There is a lot of controversy now about the doctrine of the virgin birth. Wise and cynical people refuse to believe it. Of course, it couldn't happen that way, and one very popular writer of spiritual books writes it off as a "maladroit fable." But the gentleness, the hope, the confidence is too serenely lovely to be so casually dismissed even if we don't fully understand what it's all about. The New Testament was not designed to be a textbook in obstetrics or gynecology. It is an account of God's marvelous dealings with humankind, of the passion of a God who is deeply in love with his people, and of a love which focused on Mary as a person who stood for the whole people.

What does it mean to say that Mary was simultaneously a·virgin and a mother? Does it mean that sex is evil? Does it mean that someone who came into the world through ordinary human intercourse was somehow or other more "dirty" than someone who was conceived virginally? Those who think this misunderstand completely what Matthew and Luke had in mind when they were telling their stories of the conception and birth of Jesus. Mary, the mother who was a virgin, the virgin who was a mother, is not a sign of the evilness of sex but of the goodness of God (who is responsible for sex just as he is for everything else in the world).

We must understand that Jesus was the new Adam, the beginning of a new humanity, the father of the first human race. With Jesus a fresh new start was made. Humankind was given a chance to begin all over again. Just as the beginning of the human race was a marvelous, spectacular event, the result of the direct intervention of God, so its new beginning is a marvelous and spectacular event, the result of a direct intervention of God. God created, now re-creates; he breathed life into Adam, and what was begun by the Holy Spirit was wiped out by human sin but now begins again. We all have a second chance.

It seems natural that the early church would decide to celebrate this new creation, this second chance, just at that time of the year when, with the return of the sun and the lengthening of the days, we get another chance; life begins again on earth, spring will come, and the light comes back into the world with the winter solstice and promises spring. With the conception and birth of Jesus, light came back to the human race and promised spring without end. Our ancestors went wild at the winter solstice (which in Rome became the great festive celebration of the Saturnalia), so we should go wild with joy at Christmastime because with Christ our light came into the world.

We all have a second chance. Just as Mary the virgin mother brought Jesus into the world, we also have a second chance. We can all begin again; indeed every day of our lives we can begin again. But there is no more appropriate time to begin anew than Christmas, the time when the light comes back into the world.

52

Now at this time Caesar Augustus issued a decree for a census of the whole world to be taken. This census—the first—took place while Quirinius was governor of Syria, and everyone went to his own town to be registered. So Joseph set out from the town of Nazareth in Galilee and traveled up to Judaea, to the town of David called Bethlehem, since he was of David's House and line, in order to be registered together with Mary, his betrothed, who was with child. While they were there the time came for her to have her child, and she gave birth to a son, her first-born. She wrapped him in swaddling clothes, and laid him in a manger because there was no room for them at the inn. In the countryside close by there were shepherds who lived in the fields and took it in turns to watch their flocks during the night. The angel of the Lord appeared to them and the glory of the Lord shone round them. They were terrified, but the angel said, "Do not be afraid. Listen, I bring you news of great joy, a joy to be shared by the whole people. Today in the town of David a savior has been born to you; he is Christ the Lord. And here is a sign for you: you will find a baby wrapped in swaddling clothes and lying in a manger." And suddenly with the angel there was a great throng of the heavenly host, praising God and singing:

> "Glory to God in the highest heaven,
> and peace to men who enjoy his favor."

Luke 2:1-14

225

WE know that Christmas has begun when we turn the Christmas tree lights on. The last ornament is hung, the last bit of tinsel arranged, and the big moment comes: The plug is put into the socket, the Christmas tree comes alive, and the soft, mellow, colored lights of the Christmas season fill the room. After a day or two, we are used to the tree and turning the lights on each evening becomes automatic. Still, every time the tree glows with light there is still a trace of surprise and mystery, for the room in which the tree stands appears to be a different place. Before, it was an ordinary, commonplace room; now it becomes the Christmas room.

The best Christmases of all were when we were little children. Time moved more slowly then and we had much longer to anticipate Christmas. The Christmas season was full of surprises. The displays in the store windows, the lights going up outside the houses, the purchase of the Christmas tree, mysterious packages coming into the house, the eager anticipation of presents the last days before the feast itself, when we could hardly wait. The holly, the wreaths, the pretty Christmas wrapping paper, and finally the dash to our pile of good things under the tree. There may have been a bit of a letdown when the day was over, for nothing could ever be as good in reality as we thought it would be in anticipation. Still, it was a great and glorious day, a numinous day, a day of mystery, of wonder, of awe and of surprises.

In our grown-up Christmas time, there is little surprise left. Everything has become flat, bland, predictable. The same Christmas card list, give or take a few names, the same last-minute rush, the same stresses and strains in family life, the same people at the same parties, the same uncomfortable feeling of having too much to eat and drink, the same unpleasant feeling that time is slipping through our fingers, the same vague and aimless disappointments on January 2, and, oh yes, the same football teams monopolizing the TV screen with the same breathless announcers waxing enthusiastic about the "fierce titans." It is like a bad late-night movie; we've seen it before, but we're too bored and depressed to get up and turn it off. There are occasional twinges out of the past, occasional brief remembrances of what Christmas used to be, and brief glimpses of what it could be if only there were time to think about it, time to appreciate it, time to enjoy it. If only we were still capable of finding in Christmas the surprise, the mystery, the wonder that we had as little children.

The whole point about Christmas is that something wonderful did happen. The greatest surprise in all the history of the universe really did occur. If we have grown to weary, so blase, so cynical, so sophisticated that nothing surprises us, nothing stirs us out of our routine, nothing catches us short, nothing ignites spontaneous joy or enthusiasm in our hearts, then we cannot enjoy Christmas because we are not enjoying life. The name of the Christmas game is mystery, surprise, wonder, expectation, awe. It is a time every year when we can become little children once again, when absolutely everything in the season conspires to make possible a healthy, invigorating, exciting return to childhood—not to the pettiness, the selfishness, the temper tantrums and the rivalries of childhood but to childhood's capacity for surprise. At Christmas time we become capable once again of experiencing the numinous, the marvelous, the wonderful.

What does it take to be surprised? How can we approach Christmas with the same eager expectation that we had when we were children? You can only be surprised if you believe in the possibility of unexpected good things. If you don't think that anything wonderful or marvelous could ever happen again in your life, then you never will be surprised. If the universe is not a place where wonderful and marvelous things can happen, then the coming of Jesus in Bethlehem is just one more bit of monotony and routine, one more child born into the world—hardly anything to get excited about. But if you have a child's capacity to half-expect the unexpected, then mysterious powers are still at work in the universe and in your life; and Jesus who came to us at Bethlehem can come today as well.

Has there been any wonder or surprise or spiritual excitement so far this Christmas for us? If not, should we not set aside some time before this day is over to get our spiritual heads screwed on straight and remember what it is that we are really celebrating?